ENDORSEMENTS

When I read books of extraordinary encounters and experiences, I find it greatly encouraging to know something about the author. In this case, I know Jodie personally. As I review the extraordinary experiences contained in this book, I am able to reflect on an ordinary, and if I may say, very normal, fun-loving, God-loving woman.

Not only this, but I have been with Jodie at high moments, times of challenge, and have spoken to her in the midst of a crisis. It is this knowledge that enables me to give a confident endorsement to what she has written, because her faith and walk with God doesn't change. Jodie is an adventurer, a pursuer, a persevering daughter of the King who accesses authority, wisdom, and strength in many ways. This book is not an invitation to copy her, but to be inspired and upgraded on your journey because of her example.

Because I know how "normal" Jodie is, the extraordinary has another level of impact: raw but integrous, supernatural but applicable, and heavenly but with earthly application. May your adventure begin and your expectation of an extraordinary life be upgraded.

PAUL MANWARING
Bethel Church
Author of *What On Earth is Glory*, *Kisses From a Good God*, and *Things Fathers Do*

This book is a powerful key for this era we have entered into. It is an invitation for God's people to understand their position as sons and daughters of the King and rise up in His unlimited authority to see Heaven invade earth! Jodie's teaching brings revelation that will equip and empower the saints to see their circumstances overruled and situations transformed. Her personal and powerful testimonies infuse faith and leave the reader hungry for more of God. I felt the manifest presence of God continually flood the room as I read these words—this book is anointed and dripping with impartation. I cannot recommend this book enough; it should be required reading for everyone who longs to walk more intimately with the King and see our world transformed for His glory!

LANA VAWSER
Lana Vawser Ministries
Author of *The Prophetic Voice of God*

Jodie Hughes stands as one of my heroes in the halls of faith. Rarely does one find such holy courage and perseverance on the pathway of her level of pain and sickness. In *The King's Decree,* Jodie retells the stories of triumphing over life-threatening circumstances and contending for new levels of God-encounters. This book serves as an inspiration and essential guide for anyone whose reality does not match the level of their promises.

DAN (Dano) McCOLLAM
Founding Director, Sounds of the Nations and
the Prophetic Company in Vacaville, California,
Cofounder, Bethel School of the Prophets

I have seen firsthand how God uses Jodie. *The King's Decree* will impart faith for breakthrough, inspire hope in hard and long-term circumstances, and ignite fire in your prayer life. This book will teach you how to pray effective prayers. *The King's Decree*—real life supernatural results based on real life supernatural experiences. Jodie is the real deal and I cannot recommend this book enough.

WARD SIMPSON
President, GOD TV

I was thrilled to meet Jodie Hughes for the first time on the set of God TV in Orlando, Florida. The moment she opened her mouth and displayed her beautiful accent, I took notice. Why? Like Jodie, I too have experienced the intercessory terrain of Australia. I knew that I knew she was someone who could pray through and break through the most difficult prayer assignments. And now, having read her book, *The King's Decree,* I felt the fire coming off the pages. That's not hype or cliché, but the absolute truth. There is fire in this book and you need to read it from front to back—and then all over again. Even better, get several copies and share them with your friends. You'll never be the same.

JENNIFER EIVAZ
Founder, Harvest Ministries International
Author, *Prophetic Secrets and Glory Carriers*

Jodie has personally walked through powerful truths in *The King's Decree.* Thus these teachings have been tried and proven true through the fire of her trial. Now Jodie's breakthrough can become your breakthrough! As you read through each chapter, you will tap into the heart of the Father and the power of Heaven to shift your circumstances and create victory in every area of your life!

KATIE SOUZA
Katie Souza Ministries

F.F. Bosworth said, "Faith begins where the will of God is known." This book will help you understand what the will of God is for your life and embolden you to partner with Heaven by teaching you how to make powerful, life-giving decrees. *The King's Decree* is a powerful tool for releasing breakthrough in your life. Jodie Hughes shares with such vulnerability and authenticity that it will inspire you to lean in and listen to the Lord, and then to open your mouth and decree with holy confidence what the will of the Lord is. Jodie's journey has been such an amazing series of life-threatening situations, and this book is filled with testimonies of genuine breakthrough as Jodie has made Heaven-inspired decrees to shift her circumstances. This is an important and powerful message that will encourage and inspire you no matter the situation.

KATHERINE RUONALA
Author of *Speak Life, Supernatural Freedom,*
Living in the Miraculous, Wilderness to
Wonders, and *Life with the Holy Spirit*
Senior Leader, Glory City Church Network
Founder and Facilitator of the
Australian Prophetic Council

You are holding within your hands a weapon. It is a spiritual weapon in the hands (and mouth) of whomever will run with it. Not the kind of weaponry that destroys humanity, but the revelations within this book are a weapon of mass destruction to the enemy. I find it powerfully significant that in its time of release in the Hebraic year of 5780, the number 80 in Hebrew represents the letter *pey,* which symbolically means mouth, word, expression, and speech. This tells me that this book was destined to be written in this very moment in time for the hour at hand. I can think of no greater teacher on the subject, than Jodie.

We have personally known both Ben and Jodie for many years and we can tell you that they burn for Jesus—in public and in the secret place. They are true burning ones. Jodie's words in this book have been lived out and forged in fire. You are reading living testimony, and the testimony of Jesus is the Spirit of prophecy. We encourage you, just as we have been set aflame in reading her words, to run with the burning flame of the testimony of Jesus that will be passed through the pages of this book and release a mighty decree. It's time to see Jesus unveiled through your decrees.

CHRISTY and NATE JOHNSTON
everydayrevivalists.com

God is always searching for friends He can trust, by which history may be made. Jodie Hughes is not only a friend of God, she is both a revivalist and a reformer who has seen the course of history shift by the power of her friendship that issues forth decrees from the very heart of God. Scripture teaches that *"rulers decree justice"* (Proverbs 8:15), and Jodie knows God, lives under His authority, and sees justice released on the earth as a result. In her book *The King's Decree,* you will not only be inspired by her heart-wrenching, life-changing stories, but you will also be equipped and empowered to live out the God-given authority that He has placed on your life, so you might see victorious breakthrough in every area. We highly encourage you to read this book, be drawn into the King's quarters, and receive a fresh impartation of faith and power in your life!

JERAME and MIRANDA NELSON
Elisha Revolution
Hosts of The Fire & Glory Outpouring
Authors of Burning Ones, Take Your Place
in the Kingdom, and Manifesting God's Love
through Signs, Wonders & Miracles.

It gives both Daniel and me the greatest pleasure to endorse this book, *The King's Decree,* by Jodie Hughes. We have known Jodie and Ben Hughes over many years. What impresses us the most about Jodie is not only her zeal, passion, and heart she carries for Jesus through the good times, but also the great courage and bravery she displays in the face of extremely difficult times.

We love the rawness and vulnerability of *The King's Decree;* there is something in this book to strengthen and encourage everyone. As you read through these pages you will see Jodie's determination and grit to intentionally put Jesus first in each circumstance.

The King's Decree is not just a book, we believe it's an amazing key to see radical transformation in your own life and circumstances. It doesn't matter what you are facing, you can be assured there is a decree for you written within these pages. Great hope is poured out onto each page, giving us a wonderful reminder of God's kindness and tender mercies toward us.

In *The King's Decree* we see God come through over and above with each breakthrough testimony. We see the display of the Lord's strong arm of deliverance and glory—a sweet reminder that nothing is too hard for our God. No matter what afflictions we face here on this earth, our God is always fighting for us every step of the way.

DANIEL AND CHELSEA HAGEN
Founders and Overseers of Fire Church
Ministries, Melbourne, Australia
Directors of Awakening Europe and Awakening Australia

It is an honor and privilege to endorse this book written by my dear friend, Jodie Hughes. Within these pages you will find real-life stories and deep truths that will inspire and empower your Christian walk. I have known Jodie for many years and she is a rare, unique person who never quits or backs down from any attack, but instead boldly decrees. I have seen her overcome crippling sickness that would destroy the average person, and walk out of the hospital time and time again defying the doctors' reports. She is a woman of warfare and knows how to put the enemy on the run. The authority Jodie carries changes spiritual atmospheres.

I love how real this book is and how it's not just empty words but proven revelation from the throne of God. It is a book you will want to go back to and reread when you find yourself in the valleys of life—and it will inspire you to overcome your obstacles. I pray you get much-needed insight as you read and enjoy *The King's Decree*.

CHRIS HARVEY, Revivalist

"So all this was done that it might be fulfilled which was spoken by the Lord through the prophet..." (Matthew 1:22 NKJV). To be a spokesperson for the King requires being trusted by the King to say what He is saying. Jodie Hughes' book imparts both the heart and the actions that equip the believer for the call to be a spokesperson for the King. Jodie has given her life to hearing and speaking the words of the Lord. No one I know is more qualified to lead us to *"incline your ear"* to the voice of the Lord. I highly recommend this book.

LARRY TAYLOR, Revivalist
Pastor, Oasis of Grace, Graham, Texas
Author of *Latter House Glory*

There is more power in our words than I think we even daily realize. Through this beautiful book, my friend Jodie Hughes shares her own personal story of contending for breakthrough and her health that I know will encourage you if you find yourself in a battle today! Be encouraged and empowered to speak the resurrection power of the Cross over yourself and be completely healed and set free from every affliction. Jesus is ENOUGH!

ANA WERNER
Seer and Author of *The Seer's Path*
anawerner.org

THE

KING'S
DECREE

THE

KING'S
DECREE

Throne Room Declarations that
Release Supernatural Answers to Prayer

Jodie Hughes

DESTINY IMAGE® PUBLISHERS, INC.

P.O. Box 310, Shippensburg, PA 17257-0310

"Promoting Inspired Lives."

This book and all other Destiny Image and Destiny Image Fiction books are available at Christian bookstores and distributors worldwide.

Cover design by Eileen Rockwell
Interior design by Terry Clifton

For more information on foreign distributors, call 717-532-3040.

Reach us on the Internet: www.destinyimage.com.

ISBN 13 TP: 978-0-7684-5269-3
ISBN 13 eBook: 978-0-7684-5270-9
ISBN 13 HC: 978-0-7684-5272-3
ISBN 13 LP: 978-0-7684-5271-6

For Worldwide Distribution, Printed in the U.S.A.

2 3 4 5 6 7 8 / 24 23 22 21 20

DEDICATION

For my King Jesus, my loyal Friend, who has never let me down. I live to hear You say, "Well done good and faithful servant." But what drives me even more is the thought that when I see You, I will say, "I wish I gave You more."

ACKNOWLEDGMENTS

Books are written in our hearts, and lived out in our lives, long before words are ever written on a page. In this process there are those who help write victories in your life through their sacrificial, persevering prayer that later become the stories we tell that inspire others. These ones are the unnamed heroes, a countless many whom I acknowledge that without your prayers, there would be no book. In Heaven I'll thank you all in person, but for now, my prayer warrior friends, if you have prayed for me—then my prayer is that multiplied breakthrough is returned to you. I am eternally thankful for you.

To Ben, my husband, and Keely, our daughter, you are the most precious of gifts from the King to me. I love you beyond words. You are not just part of my stories, you are the joy of my heart and the catalysts of breakthroughs that the true impact of which will be told in Heaven.

Ben, Keely, and Lauren, our adopted-into-our-family spiritual daughter, thank you all for helping make this book possible with your surrendered lives and your tireless help that made the process fun. I love you bunches. What a journey! And the best is yet to come.

CONTENTS

A Note from Jodie

JESUS.

I struggled to find an appropriate opening line for a book that has taken far too many years to finally get on paper. But there's only one word, one name, one person who deserves the honor of the first word, and that's Jesus.

So as I kick off, I'm compelled to say, I'm thankful to Jesus, my King and my Friend. To be able to walk you through my heart and share these stories of wild encounters, powerful declarations, and impartation of fire from the throne room, is my joy. Jesus gets my standing ovation, thunderous applause, and thanks. He deserves all the glory for every word written, every heart that is impacted, and every miracle that follows.

Nothing is impossible, my friend, even that which looks impossible right now.

Be ready for the God of the miraculous to speak life, hope and destiny doors opening for you. God is releasing supernatural answers that accelerate promise as *"No weapon formed against you will succeed"* (Isaiah 54:17 CSB).

How do I know this?

It's by *The King's Decree*,

—JODIE xo

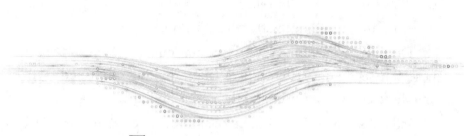

FOREWORD

By Shawn Bolz

Throughout human history we have seen the impact of the spiritual declarations wielded by Christians who have passionate faith in God. These declarations, and the life behind them, have huge impact to shape societies, set culture, provide heritage, and bring vision for the future. Jodie's book, *The King's Decree,* is a very specific tool to help you use words to define your own history and future with God.

I love the power of hearing others' faith stories and then using both the Word and our own prayers to declare. These have been weapons in my own life to create the context of faith and intimacy in which I am now living.

Prayer helps us to commune with God's nature and heart. We get to converse with God with listening ears. We get to share our pain, victory, struggles, and inner life with God. Through prayer, we allow the Holy Spirit to share with us space in God's heart, and we experience being one with Him each time.

Declarations are when we speak out loud *on* purpose *for* purpose. These are our statements of faith, aligning us to God's will and directives for our lives and the world around us.

Jodie uses many beautiful verses to illustrate her points, but I want to highlight one she used: Life is in the power of the tongue: *"Death and life are in the power of the tongue, and those who love it will eat its fruit"* (Proverbs 18:21 NKJV). As a Christian and as an emotionally intelligent human, we see that the tongue is our most powerful tool or weapon. It has power to release life wherever we go. People who understand this will speak intentionally and will eat the abundant fruit their past words, declarations, have produced.

I wrote in my own prayer devotional book, *Breakthrough,* and included declarations in each chapter because I so believe in this principle and theology. One of the keys I write about in *Breakthrough* is that we will speak to others, and to ourselves, because we realize that silence is indifference and passivity is a thief. We speak out what is inside to align our outside world with God's truths.

Declarations help us to be intentional and therefore more aware of when God does move, because we are declaring, and then looking for the fulfillment of very specific statements.

It is time to develop words that you can use to cultivate faith in your identity, calling, and destiny.

We see lots of Scripture examples of people using prophetic words, prayers, and declarations as an articulated tool in their relationship to their faith and connection to God, themselves, and the world.

Through Jodie's book she is inviting you to use words to speak into the very fabric of your life, the spiritual realm, and the world around you.

Jodie and her family have been on a very radical journey with so many supernatural encounters that it might even seem a little overwhelming to read, let alone believe that her life could be an example of faith for you. But after you read this, faith will come by hearing the principles of declaration, the theology of what she is writing about, and ultimately the stories she tells.

This really is a series of encounters that create an incredible picture of Jodie's inner process with God. I felt when reading her encouragements and declarations that God was using them to ultimately create an example for us of how to have our identity so deeply connected to our relational process with God.

I got so much out of this book. I have known Jodie for many years, but in reading this book it feels more like sitting down and having a mentoring conversation about deep spiritual faith, than it does just an inspirational book. Settle into a cozy spot and get ready to embrace or sharpen the tool of declaration in your own life.

SHAWN BOLZ
Podcast host of *Exploring the Prophetic*
TV host of *Translating God* on TBN and
Exploring the Industry on CBN
Author of *Translating God, Breakthrough
Prophecies, Prayers & Declarations*

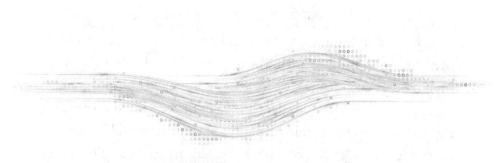

PREFACE

*...Open your mouth with a mighty decree; I will fulfill it
now, you'll see! The words that you speak, so shall it be!*
—Psalm 81:10 TPT

There are many voices in life, many opinions, influences, and noise that clutters our thinking. But there is only one voice that carries supernatural hope and resurrection power to actually transform our circumstances. Partnering with Heaven to release on earth what God is saying from the throne room is a game changer. I have walked through many "valleys of the darkest shadows" as I call them, and always have I encountered the God of the feasting table in the midst of the enemy's schemes. My King has faithfully decreed light to the darkness, breakthrough to the obstacles, and life where death thought it had won. Leaning in to hear what God is speaking, and then decreeing that, unleashes the power of the *"mighty decree…The words that you speak, so shall it be!"*

I believe in the God of the impossible because I've seen Him over and over again show up in my life. Often it's been in wild, supernatural encounters that have brought needed breakthroughs, right at the moment I needed it. Many of these wild encounters showed me the crucial role we play in partnering with Heaven and decreeing into existence that which we haven't seen yet. The power of the "mighty decree" from our own mouth is not to be understated, or under-utilized! History is being written, even as I write these pages, by those who know their authority in God and just won't quit!

The King's Decree will stir contagious fire, hope where you need it most, and faith for more of God. But it will also release new fire on your voice and decrees that will open destiny doors. You are poised for unprecedented outbreaks of greater glory, and this book will empower you and release "now faith." It's "take off" season for the promises God is speaking from the throne room.

I'm aware many are facing challenging circumstances, and walking through places of disappointment, process, or delay. I also know many are boldly taking on modern-day giants and shaping our generation with anointed courage. I understand contending and believing for what you haven't seen yet. And I salute the incredible perseverance and radical faith of the church I am seeing arise after walking through devastating seasons, and yet still overcoming.

Whether you walked in "valleys of the shadow" or climbed mountains that required fierce determination, this book is written for you, my friend. Your desire to seek the heart of the King, pursue His glory and supernatural breakthrough, and run hard after the more of God, is what gives many, including me, great faith that the Church is entering our finest hour.

I'm equally aware that for many there is often a mix of challenging circumstances and breakthrough happening all at once. One front can be a constant battle, while another area of our lives is breaking through into new heights of victory, requiring us to run purposefully into unprecedented favor, trusting God as we go. Living in the tension of seemingly opposing circumstances while keeping our hearts burning after God is "real" life.

There is always more. There is always hope. Believing these two truths is the first key to breakthrough. There are divine solutions for every obstacle and every question.

This book is an edict of hope, an impartation of fire, and the real person's guide to decrees that bring breakthrough in our actual lives, the places we live, and in the situations we think there is no way forward. There is no shortage of hope in Heaven, and the King of kings is always decreeing divine answers custom-made for you and the nations. There is an intercession revolution taking place right now, as those who have walked through the fire are arising in hard-fought victories and new authority. There is deep knowing in these ones that they are born and positioned for this very hour, and their voices are catalysts of hope.

The King's Decree is an announcement of hope and equally a call to action. This is not an hour of retreat or demise, it is instead the hour of our greatest breakthroughs. Those giants that have long intimidated, are being silenced as pivotal change is established in prayer. Decrees that release supernatural solutions, that once spoken shift everything, are reshaping our communities, families, and nations.

You are invited into a journey that activates greater faith to shift circumstances and releases miracles. There's a divine explosion of accelerated power and mountain-leveling faith that happens when we combine Heaven's truths with our childlike expectation, and speak forth change.

God is using our lives and our journeys to speak His heart right where we are. All of us are empowered and powerful when we are being ourselves. You are the voice in your world that God is using.

I had a powerful encounter many years ago when I was trying desperately hard in ministry to "get it right," whatever that really means. I heard God say as I was stressing myself out from trying to be all I thought I should be, *"Jodie, it's you I called, and it's you I want you to be, and it's you I need you to be. Never be afraid to be you!"* (That may be a word for you too.) What God told me changed everything from that moment on. I resolved I didn't need to be like everyone else or do ministry like others; in fact, the most anointed version of me, is the authentic me.

It's the same for us all—God anoints original. There is great freedom in life, family, and ministry when we just be ourselves! And so, this is how I'm writing my book, me on a page.

So with that said, you won't find this book full of perfection, line upon line of exegesis, uncompassionate faith, or neat, tidy stories. But you *will* find this book full of wild encounters, authenticity, a real journey filled with grace, stories that contain raw pain and life-saving miracles, and the very real miracle-releasing, resurrection power of Jesus.

No battle is without pain. But these pages are *not* ultimately about pain or struggle—they are about the King who decrees life, and miracle solutions follow. These pages represent hard-fought-for victories and supernatural interventions; but ultimately, it's the story of our King who decrees breakthrough. Never allow what the enemy has thrown at you to prophesy your future or define who you are, as you are defined by the voice of the King.

My prayer is that these stories, encounters, and supernatural keys resonate deeply, no matter what you are walking through, and impart the same divine answers, and contagious fire in your heart.

In these pages you will find:

- Decrees that activate change and miracles.
- Prayer, impartation, and blessing from the throne room.
- Divine strategy that releases new authority on *your* voice.
- Stories of wild encounters that release supernatural keys and breakthrough.
- Keys to equip you to partner with God as you decree.
- Contagious fire and impartation of resurrection life.
- Hope that unlocks your voice as you contend.
- Supernatural answers to real circumstances in your life.

Every encounter and story I share is an invitation for the same breakthrough in your life. Some of my stories may stretch you, some may provoke you; but I believe raw faith will be provoked so that you are anointed, and fresh heart connection to Jesus will be stirred.

You'll read stories of:

- Eleventh-hour breakthroughs

- Angels suddenly appearing in hospital rooms and my bedroom
- Lazarus suddenlies
- God taking over my TV and prophesying a word to me
- Supernatural lights appearing in the night that brought justice
- Visions of family being escorted to Heaven
- Revival breakouts
- Honey manifesting in my prayer room
- Rain that healed me
- God's audible voice
- Decrees that brought miraculous change
- And much more

I have prayed over every word you will read in this book, and I'm expectant for *your breakthrough*. I believe with you, friend, that as you read *The King's Decree,* God's presence will manifest tangibly and you will not finish this book the same as you began it.

God used the wild encounters I've had to reinforce the importance and power of partnering with the King as we decree truth to our circumstances, and then impart the same breakthroughs to others. One encounter in particular—when an angel suddenly showed up in my hospital room when, to be honest, I was really in serious trouble without God stepping in—made it clear to me just how powerful our decrees are. This angel brought a list of the promises over my life from the throne room that I had decreed over my life. I won't ruin what happened next as you will read about it later, but I tell you now, our declarations are powerful and they move the unseen to the seen.

Our lives are practically and powerfully impacted when we declare what God is saying. God made this point loud and clear when I was desperately unwell one time, and not recovering from emergency bowel surgery. After prayer, I had a vision of a "flaming red train track," and I immediately knew it was a tract of infection—a fissure that had not been found in the previous surgery. Doctors agreed I needed another emergency surgery to find any additional tiny fissures of infection from my intestines but admitted this was incredibly difficult, like finding a "needle in a haystack," but also urgent as I was rapidly deteriorating.

As God had already revealed the issue to us, my husband and I prayed and decreed *"light"* to guide the surgeons. The surgery was successful, praise God—but what the surgeon told us afterward was astounding! He said, "I searched all around your intestines and I couldn't find the tract of infection anywhere. Then suddenly a *flash of light* appeared inside your body, so I looked where the light flashed, and I found the fissure of infection!" What?! Wow! God literally flashed light inside my body to reveal it! I knew again that God was saying our prayers are powerful. Our decrees indeed move the unseen to the seen, and shift Heaven's solutions to earth.

God is most certainly still the God of Lazarus, turning the impossible around, and He wants us to live in this truth in our everyday lives, so our circumstances are influenced by throne room solutions and God's word, more than the voices of fear and confusion. More to the point, Kingdom decrees change things. We all have promises recorded in Heaven, we all have an Advocate in God our King, and we all have need of supernatural answers available. The good news is, God is very good at His job! Our voice is not insignificant or unheard in Heaven—our decrees are mighty and they activate the armies of Heaven and resurrection power every time we believe and decree what God is saying!

The power of life is carried by our mouths, and God invites us to partner with Him. This is astounding! This is breathtaking. May we be compelled to decree a thing and be part of seeing God's dreams established in not just our own lives, but generations to come.

Many known prophetic voices such as Lana Vawser, Shawn Bolz, Stacey Campbell, and Miranda and Jerame Nelson, have prophesied this book that reveals inner battles, enemy assaults, and wild supernatural encounters that changed everything for me. I've never shared them all in one title or laid out the raw battle behind the breakthroughs and the wisdom graciously imparted to contend and decree. These keys to decree from the throne room have brought not just breakthrough to me, but impart-able breakthrough whenever I release them. I pray the same for you—that the anointing of God would leap off these very pages as you read. It's time, my friend, it's *your* time for breakthrough.

These same prophetic words all prophesied that when I released a book it would carry impartation of miracles. So with this, I boldly decree miracle breakthroughs over your life. The God of the impossible is very much alive and decreeing miracle turnarounds and unparalleled victories for you.

The season ahead is uncharted territory, but it's what we are made for. We're on the cusp of the greatest days of harvest and revival fire we have ever seen. There's a rising urgency to impact history, and for all of us to be walking, talking mobile decrees of the King on assignment wherever we go.

No situation is beyond the reach of our King. No circumstance is without hope. No mountain exists that isn't subject to the decree of the King. I hope this is more than a book for you; books come and go, but decrees that come from God echo into eternity, effecting generations to come.

Be expectant as you *"Open your mouth with a mighty decree. ... The words that you speak, so shall it be!"* (Psalm 81:10 TPT).

How do I know?

It's by *The King's Decree.*

MY PRAYER FOR YOU

I thank God for you and I bless you. I speak forth an atmosphere of hope and expectancy around you as you read these pages, and I ask King Jesus for miracle turnarounds where you need it. Nothing is impossible with God, including what looks impossible right now—and so I pray breakthrough. I ask God to come and meet you right in the middle of "that situation" you are walking through even now. No weapon formed against you shall prosper, and I command every assignment of the enemy to be broken.

I speak God's tangible presence around you, fresh connection of your heart to His, and contagious hunger after God stirred anew. You are made for greatness and God is leading you out of the grave and into redeemed stories. Every victory I have walked in, every door of kindness God has opened, and every encounter that has restored hope and life, I release the same to you, my friend.

THE KING'S DECREE

I bless your mouth to speak mighty decrees that release Heaven on earth. I bless your destiny and promises with resurrection life by decree of the King.
Amen.

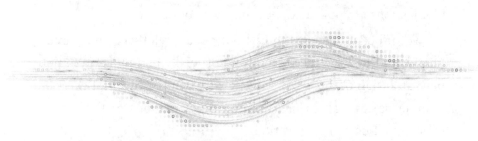

INTRODUCTION

By Patricia King

A *decree* is different from a confession or proclamation, even though all may contain some similar content.

When you confess, you are admitting, acknowledging, testifying, or stating a personal belief. We find this word used in Romans 10:9 (NASB): *"that if you confess with your mouth Jesus as Lord, and believe in your heart that God raised Him from the dead, you will be saved."*

We see the word "confess" also used in the area of making confession of our sins: *"If we confess our sins, He is faithful and righteous to forgive us our sins and to cleanse us from all unrighteousness"* (1 John 1:9 NASB).

Confessions can be private as in a counseling situation, or in public such as a courtroom, public baptism, or speaking platform. Confessions are powerful, but they are not decrees.

To "proclaim" means to call out, recite, read, cry out, publish, herald, and to announce something officially and most often publicly. In Isaiah 61:1-2 we discover that when the Spirit of the Lord is upon us, we can bring anointed proclamations of the truth—official, public communication.

> The Spirit of the Lord God is upon me, because the Lord has anointed me to bring good news to the afflicted; He has sent me to bind up the brokenhearted, to proclaim liberty to captives and freedom to prisoners; to proclaim the favorable year of the Lord and the day of vengeance of our God; to comfort all who mourn (Isaiah 61:1-2 NASB).

In Mark 1:43 when the leper was cleansed by Jesus, he was warned by Jesus not to tell anyone but rather to show himself to the priest according to the law, in order to be officially declared clean. Instead the man went forth and made a big public announcement: "But he went out and began to proclaim it freely and to spread the news around..." (Mark 1:45 NASB).

A *decree* is different from both a confession and a proclamation in that it is brought forth through governmental initiation and it carries much more authority than a confession or proclamation. A decree is an official command or judicial order issued by a legal, governmental authority.

> ...write as you see fit, in the king's name, and seal it with the king's signet ring—for a decree which is written in the king's name and sealed with the king's signet ring may not be revoked (Esther 8:8 AMP).

This is remarkable when you understand that Jesus holds the keys to the highest governmental authority in the universe and for all eternity. If God said it, you can believe it—and that will settle it! The words of Jesus are *"spirit and life"* (John 6:63); and as you decree them in faith, they do not return void but will accomplish what they are sent to do (Isaiah 55:11).

I have loved decrees of God's Word since I was a fairly new believer. I believe that decrees are one of the most powerful tools we've been given for our growth in the Lord for effective prayer and warfare, and for calling Heaven's will into manifestation on earth.

In *The King's Decree*, Jodie Hughes so beautifully inspires the reader to step into the exercise of decrees. Her testimonies and examples will build your faith, while her teaching segments woven in and through the content are easy to understand and follow. This book will truly empower you to adequately and efficiently decree the Word in order to bring life-transforming shifts, miracles, and glorious manifestations of God's goodness into your life. You will also discover a wonderful mystery—*you* are the King's decree!

I love the King. I love decrees. I love Jodie Hughes…and I love this book!

Chapter 1

MORE THAN WORDS

You will also decree a thing, and it will be established for you....
—JOB 22:28 NASB

The King's decree is more than just words. It's an ongoing conversation, an invitation to know the King Himself, to listen, partner, announce, collaborate, and speak. It's the call to effect change, to be the artist's paintbrush, the musician's instrument, the Father's heart, Heaven's voice—the King's decree.

To hear God and decree on behalf of the King, releasing declarations that effect our surroundings and circumstances, is mind-blowing. But it's also an extension and natural flow of an ongoing communication between two friends. One of us just happens to be the King! When the King says something, it carries a higher authority than other voices in our life. When the King speaks, earth listens.

I believe words create new realities. I live my life like this. When I talk about this I never want to convey a sense of condemnation or religious nitpicking about what and how we say things, as that is *not* what I'm talking about.

Yes, God upgrades our speech at times; but the thing is, God is upgrading our understanding that our very lives are a declaration, and that we are all atmosphere releasers and shifters. I can release an atmosphere of faith or an atmosphere of fear based on my words, conversations, and what's coming from my heart. I have learned to choose what atmosphere I want to live under. I *need* to enthrone God in my praises and decrees, and even my personal conversations that are behind closed doors, because I *need* an atmosphere of faith, miracles, and God's manifest presence in my life just so I can "do life."

Before we go any further, let's acknowledge afresh our need to hear the voice of God. Just simply say, "My God and my King, I need You and I want to hear You with greater clarity." This is a prayer God answers.

AN AUSSIE GIRL

I'm proud to be an Aussie girl who currently lives in Texas in the United States, but I'm Australian through and through. I actually say things like "crikey," "arvo" (afternoon), and "Yeah nah" (Yes, but no. Said with a smile.). I grew up on Vegemite and Tim Tams, and I miss my pub-style chicken schnitzel. I can't survive without "flat whites," Australia's favorite coffee. And seeing a beach is life to me, not just a nice vacation. I love that I come from the Great Southland of the Holy Spirit, which is the prophetic name for Australia that is decreed passionately as Australia's birthright and destiny.

I love the "realness" of my Australian culture, and the way as a nation we have a spirit that is known as the "Aussie Battlers." I prefer to call it the Aussie Champions, as this does mark us as a people with courage and raw grit that is seen best "under fire." Australians carry the breaker anointing, and innately rise above when obstacles come knocking, and stand with their "mates"—we also know how to battle and have fun at the same time. It's a nation on the cusp of Awakening.

God suddenly and recently moved my family to live in the United States, another nation we have long loved. I love the honor and celebration of greatness America carries, as this encourages the pioneering spirit in a brave people. I see generosity of heart and courage to sacrificially pursue justice that inspires me and encourages entrepreneurism. We enjoy living in the state of Texas—though I know enough to know *real* Texans lovingly say the *nation* of Texas—and discovering things like brisket, ribs, and chicken-fried chicken (yes, that really is what it's called). America too is on the cusp of another great Awakening that will make all other moves of God pale in comparison.

My husband, Ben, and I have always been in ministry of some description, and our beautiful adult daughter, Keely, ministers with us too, which is so very special. Lauren, our spiritual daughter, also moved to America with us and is part of our ministry. We've been missionaries, pastors, church planters, itinerant ministers, led revivals including the Pineapple Revival on the Sunshine Coast of Australia, have launched several revival schools, online mentoring and host a TV show, but my favorite, we have been "Mum and Dad" to many. Between Ben and I, we've worked at varying churches and denominations from The Salvation Army, the Methodists, YWAM, Hillsong, to currently Pour It Out Ministries. All of this has been an honor and has given us a broad experience of the body of Christ and a deep love for *the* Church.

POUR IT OUT

Pour It Out is the ministry that Ben and I pioneered after an angel woke us up and stood on our bed in the middle of the night! A marker moment for sure. God commissioned us in this encounter from Zechariah 4 to "pour out the oil of God's presence and power." Yes, that changed our lives a *lot*. Can I say again, *a lot*. I talk more about this encounter later in the book.

That encounter left us changed by the tangible awe, wonder, and fear of the Lord that I'm so thankful for. The fear of the Lord that marked us wasn't a scared-of-God fear, it was a reverence of His holiness and an extreme awareness that holiness matters, purity matters, and character matters. It really did purge our hearts and set off a fresh "create in me a clean heart" season that was so necessary as we stepped into a new assignment of the Lord.

I believe the church is at this same juncture in the road right now, where God is calling us to *"Consecrate yourselves, for tomorrow the Lord will do amazing things among you."* (Joshua 3:5). There is a very real invitation to consecrate our hearts afresh, so we can steward well the greater glory and unprecedented harvest God is taking us into.

It's God's grace and goodness to increase the fear of the Lord before we enter promotion, as God is preparing and positioning us to walk in upgraded wisdom that stewards well the increased authority and blessing we are coming into. *"The fear of the Lord is the beginning of wisdom,"* (Proverbs 9:10). When we have encountered the fear of the Lord, it compels us to make wise decisions. All I can say is, I am so, so grateful for this encounter that changed everything. When that angel woke us up, I knew this call would cost us everything, but everything is no sacrifice at all in service of the living King.

We are in ministry as a family, and this is my greatest joy. It's also been a huge learning curve and humbling experience. It hasn't always been easy, but it's fair to say that serving God has given me my best life—and moments of exhilaration, amazement, and "fall on the ground in a heap crying" kind of thankfulness. Seeing people healed, encounter God's love, and lives radically impacted with hope and revival fire—there's nothing like it and no better life I yearn for. I'm living the life I'm made for and that's saying something. I pray this for you—to thrive in the life you're made for.

DIRECTING THE ATMOSPHERE

If you were a fly on the wall in my prayer room or watching me worship in a meeting, you'd likely see me marching back and forth pointing, and my arms flailing around. I imagine and I "visioneer" that I am directing the atmosphere, just as a conductor directs an orchestra. I imagine my arms are not limited to the end of my fingers, but they extend into the realm of "all things are possible" where God said, "Let there be light" and then there was. In this glory realm where suddenly the intangible becomes tangible, and the God of the Bible becomes a very present reality, I come alive. This is a combustion moment of God speaking and His child hearing, and a colliding of Heaven and earth. These moments change things.

The God I know is gentle and my Friend, and yet He is also fierce and formidable, as His words carry power to raise the dead. That is my God, the King of kings and Creator of the universe; and He continues to create, as any creative does. Every time you see a sunrise is evidence our Creator is still creating beauty. He sees His masterpiece and says, "It's good," and then incredibly gives authority to us to interact and paint with Him, with our words and lives. What humility first of all! What artist allows others to add their touch to an existing painting?

And what an honor to co-labor with God Himself and add a touch, a color, or a note into the song. What great composer would allow the instruments themselves to add to their masterpiece? We are empowered to collaborate with God. What humility and graciousness our Creator walks in to allow, actually commission us, to partner with Him in bringing Heaven to earth. We're invited to use our lives as instruments of redemption, adding beauty.

Collaborating, or conversing, with the King is interactive prayer. We are not simply saying words or reading Scripture or releasing prayers to speak into circumstances, we are part of the creative process and divine conversation, and our voice intrinsically becomes an instrument in the orchestral movement known as on earth as my Father says (read Matthew 6:10).

Our words, partnering with *the* Word, inextricably influence the world around us. In partnership with the King of kings, the Divine Composer, we are displacing darkness with a melody of light. This is prayer. This is a conversation with God the Creator. This is warfare. This is friendship with a King. This is declaration. *This is the King's decree!*

What God decrees today is no less powerful than when He spoke the universe into existence. Wow! Get ahold of that! God's written Word, the Bible, is active and alive (read Hebrews 4:12), and His spoken word, *rhema,* is active and alive—the written and spoken Word of God is like supernatural dynamite. A key to part-nering in this explosion of power is strangely simple: Listen for what He is saying and release the same into the world around you. Of course, read the Bible, as nothing God says violates Scripture.

Like any conversation or creative process, it's interactive. Our mouths become instruments engaging in an interactive, orches-tral masterpiece of hope shifting impossible to possible. It's warfare of the most exhilarating, beauty-focused, life-giving, redemptive kind. God is always releasing redemptive hope, even in godless, horrific situations on the earth. Listen for the redemptive notes that speak to unfinished, broken stories. He knows how to rewrite and rework any story.

KEELY'S CONVERSATION LESSONS

As you read earlier, Ben and I have always been in ministry of some description, which means our daughter, Keely, has grown up in the public eye, which is not always *fun,* but she has always had an abil-ity to thrive anywhere, and to make people feel loved and special.

When Keely was about 6 or so years old, we knew that rela-tional intelligence was as much a part of ministry as anything else, and for all of us is considered a helpful life skill. This might seem obvious, but Ben was especially determined to add to this strength in Keely's life and "speak life" to her already-confident personal-ity. To this end, he gave her "conversation lessons." Yes, you read that right! She was more than able to hold a conversation, don't get me wrong, but Ben was speaking life over her boldness and confidence. It was really cute, sometimes hilarious, and actually became a fun connection time for them.

Basically, Ben started a conversation and encouraged Keely to actively listen, ask questions to keep him talking, and lead the conversation. He encouraged her to be confident and bold in who she was and honor others. Their conversation lessons would last for ages sometimes, as Ben and Keely talked about all manner of things. It really became a fun thing they did together, and fun for me to listen to all their diverse and crazy topics. My point is, though, it is a skill that can be taught and grown.

I believe it's the same when it comes to our conversations with God. We can grow our friendship and actively grow in how we listen, hear, and recognize His voice, discerning what He's saying and focusing on His heart. As we steward our friendship and set apart time with Him, we grow together. Be encouraged, friend. We're all on a journey. And if you find chatting with God challenging or dry or boring or labored, ask the Holy Spirit to give you *conversation lessons*! I guarantee you, it won't be boring. The oil will come, I promise you. Discussions with the King are nothing if not interesting!

FRIEND TO FRIEND

As the conversation tarries with God, I realize that this is not about the words as much as it's about the ongoing conversation with a Friend and making time to know His heart, know His ways, and know what He might say before He even says it. The way God speaks, the emotion in His voice, the implied wisdom, the times when silence is not an end of a conversation, but simply a pause to emphasize a point.

Knowing God, not just *about* God, is friendship. What's distinctive about this Friend is when He speaks, the earth surrenders to His voice. Of all the birthrights He gives to us His children, He still says, *"Whoever has ears, let them hear"* (Matthew 11:15). It's our choice to make time to listen, and to just be in His presence.

I remember God whispering to me as I was in worship and just about to get up and preach one day. He said, *"I have many associates, but few friends."* Oh my goodness. I started crying. There wasn't anger in His voice, instead I sensed the heart of a King who calls us friends and desires friendship. I imagined a scene with Him waiting at some cafe for me to show up for coffee; but sadly, sometimes I left God waiting. I didn't return His calls. I didn't answer when He tried to speak to me. I didn't let Him into my heart. Some days I didn't even say hello.

God Desires Friends, not Associates

My heart was pierced by the truth that God desires friends, not associates. He wants to share His heart with us. Even as I write this I am in tears as I again am reminded that everything is about Jesus, our Friend. Everything comes from intimate connection with Him, and nothing is more important than this…nothing. Doing is important. But *being* comes first. May I *be* a friend of God.

> *"I have never called you 'servants,' because a master doesn't confide in his servants, and servants don't always understand what the master is doing. But **I call you my most intimate friends**, for I reveal to you everything that I've heard from my Father"* (John 15:15 TPT).

There's power when a friend of God speaks. Anointing flows. Glory falls. Those who have been in His presence and know Him, they speak and live differently. The King is looking for those He can trust with His authority. How do we walk in this authority? Be a friend of God. It all comes back to friendship, and the ongoing conversation between two friends, one just happens to be a King.

OUR KING IS THE VICTORY-DECREEING GOD

One of my favorite Scriptures is Psalm 44:4, *"You are my King and my God, who decrees victories for Jacob."* Our King is a victory-decreeing God! I speak over you: no matter what is going on right now, there is a victorious solution that God is speaking over you from the throne room even right now. There is a way forward and a supernatural answer that God is already decreeing.

The key is having the conversation with God, leaning into the glory realm and decreeing from the perspective of victory that Heaven is already releasing! Say out loud with me, "My God is a victory-decreeing God and He has victories and solutions for me."

Psalm 44:4 has been an anchor for me, especially when the storms of life have tried to take me out. In these times, I've needed to shut out voices that add doubt and fear, and give influence to voices that speak life, truth, and hope. I've heard it said that "those with the most hope, have the most influence." This is because those who know their God well have the most influence, because Heaven is never short of hope, *ever*!

I have spoken, prayed, decreed, cried, whispered and shouted this verse as I've marched around in hospital rooms, churches, living rooms, prayer rooms, bedrooms, beaches, and nations. I've had to marinate in this truth. I've needed to say it out loud so my own ears have heard it, and my own heart has received it.

One such time was when I had been in the hospital in an isolation ward for more than a month. The prognosis from the doctors was grim and their advice at the time was to remove half my stomach and entire bowel, which would require feeding me through a tube for the rest of my life. I had been extremely unwell, unable to digest food, and had infection and inflammation taking over my system. Doctors were concerned as I was skin and bones, very weak, with almost no immunity. This wasn't the first time I'd been hospitalized facing uncertain and scary outcomes from intestinal disease, nor was it without precedent of God miraculously healing me as He had broken through many times before, but this time there was urgent need of breakthrough to prevent drastic life-altering surgery.

I'm a minister, yes, but also a wife and Mum, and in that moment I just wanted to live out my days and go home with my family. Often in retelling my story, I tend to speak as if it's someone else's story. This is largely due to the redemption of God closing so many of these painful chapters in my life; consequently, it's been emotional, even challenging, writing this book and tapping into the rawness of times my life hung in the balance.

Keely was about to turn 12 years old, and I wanted her to have a healthy, alive Mum. I knew God had called me to the nations and I knew God as my Healer, but this was where the rubber met the road—and you find out what you really believe! I wasn't going to just wait for the surgery's outcome. I got out of bed to fight with every ounce of strength I had. I got up with the intravenous drip attached to me and went into my en suite bathroom—one benefit of being in isolation was I had my own private room and bathroom.

I shut the door, and in the tiny space available I marched around the room in circles for literally hours speaking out, "You are my King and my God who decrees victories for Jacob!" (Psalm 44:4).

Jacob had a limp from wrestling and contending with God, and that night as I limped and slowly shuffled around that bathroom, it encouraged me that the places where I *limped* I too would see victory. I shouted. I whispered. I cried. I was in extreme pain that was only exacerbated by my marching, but I knew I needed to appeal to a higher court, to the very throne room of God. *His* voice was my diagnosis. Don't hear me wrong, many were praying for me, and I had prayed much before this night, but something militant came on me in that moment. I spoke victory out over and over and over.

I remember it was in the early hours of the night, around 3 a.m., when I finally stopped and climbed into my bed, exhausted. Nothing had happened as I prayed for hours, except I absolutely knew I had stormed Heaven. I felt the same. My body was hurting so badly that tears were streaming down my face as I climbed into bed.

I had only been in bed a few moments with the lights out and my eyes closed when I felt someone tap my shoulder and gently shake me. I kept my eyes closed, as I thought it was a nurse; and honestly, I was so exhausted I thought whatever was needed could be done without me being awake. But someone tapped my shoulder again, this time more firmly, so I opened my eyes, only to realize no one was there! Yet I could still feel a firm hand on my shoulder. I immediately knew an angel was there with me. I knew the Lord in His kindness was reminding me, "I'm with you, the God who decrees victories is with you." Such a tangible peace flooded my entire body. I felt hope arise.

It was the middle of the night and dark with no lights on in my room, suddenly with my eyes open, I saw a golden ray of light shine in though my hospital door window, like morning light except brighter and more golden. As I stared at the light, it looked alive and carried an atmosphere of hope that invaded my room. Then just as suddenly, I watched golden, glorious dust, like dancing glitter or tiny golden fire embers float upon the beam of golden light and move across the room, some 3 meters (9 feet), to settle over my hospital bed.

It sounds like a Disney movie scene retelling it, but the golden, glorious dust floated over my body. My hospital room felt *alive* in God's presence. I didn't feel any physical change in my body right away, but I *knew* the God who decrees victories had visited me; and in His glory, things change.

The next thing I knew, a nurse was waking me up for real, and it was time to get ready for surgery. The great miracle outcome of that surgery was that the doctors saw enough "sudden change" to send me home a couple days later recovering instead of pursuing life-effecting surgery. A process of healing continued to miraculously unfold, and I knew my God and my King decreed a victory for me that night. He is decreeing victories for you also from the throne room right now, and I partner my voice with yours, and decree Heaven's solutions and transforming power into the places *you* need a miracle.

THE POWER OF USING OUR VOICE

In this coming era, our words are going to increasingly release incredible power. In partnership with God, our words are writing history. Those who have been with God are shaping the next season with their decrees. This is an invitation, even a trumpet-blast commissioning, to all believers.

We are in a time of great change. Change is happening swiftly, and not all of it is God-inspired. We have been given authority by God to speak forth God's heart and Heaven's strategies and solutions. Our voices *must* be heard and released. Our decrees and prayers must release God-change and cancel the voice of demonically inspired change. I really believe in the years to come that how we speak will be increasingly impacted by the level of power and authority coming on our voices.

Decreeing is not just words, it's more than words! It's not just the words in and of themselves that make declaration powerful, as words alone hold no supernatural power. Decreeing is even more than prayer. It's the faith and authority attached to the words we speak, because we know our King who makes a decree powerful. It's the Source they come from, and the faith they are spoken in that adds the power. A decree is much more than words.

Decrees are Heaven's whispers, from our future home, and so they carry power to transform the nations as they are spoken out in faith. To *"decree a thing, and it will be established for you"* (Job 22:28 NASB) is to be a son and daughter of the King, privileged to be part of a divine, unending family conversation with your heavenly Father.

Your decrees are releasing your heavenly Dad's heart, and your words are establishing it. Your world needs your voice, just as my world needs my voice, and we are commissioned to be that voice.

THE KING'S DECREE FOR YOU

"My child, what you decree with Me will be established for you. Open your mouth, let it out and watch what I will do through you."
—THE KING

MY PRAYER FOR YOU

I speak the peace of Heaven over you and bubbling expectation that God is using your life and your voice to influence and impact your world. I bless your voice. I bless your current circumstances, and I pray God's tangible presence over you. I bless your conversations with the King. I bless your ears to hear and your mouth to decree what God is saying with increased authority, establishing power in your life. God is a victory-decreeing King, and I ask for victories breaking out in you and around you, my friend, that astound and bring great joy, by decree of the King. In Jesus' name, amen.

DECREE

- I am a child of the King of kings.
- I hear my Father, the King, with great clarity, and I boldly release what He is saying.
- It is not just the words I speak that carry power, it is my authority as a child of the King and the power of Jesus' blood that transforms circumstances.

- I have authority to release Heaven on earth, and I attach faith to what I pray and decree.

- My God and my King is decreeing victory for me right now, and He has throne-room solutions for me.

- With the authority of the King, I decree victory over every area of my life.

Chapter 2

THE KING'S MOUTHPIECE

My sheep hear My voice, and I know
them, and they follow Me.
—John 10:27 NKJV

I know God is the God of supernatural answers because I've seen them happen in my own life over and over and over again. I've prayed for many people over the years and have seen my hero, King Jesus, show up and do wild, "impossible" things.

I'll never forget many years ago praying for a lady who looked to be six months pregnant, only to discover her stomach was swollen due to bowel disease. She said, "I don't know if you can understand how I feel." Her words evoked compassion; and with tears in my eyes, I replied, "Actually I really do understand." As I prayed, before our eyes, in maybe sixty seconds, her stomach shrunk back to normal size and all pain left her body! My Jesus—your Jesus—can do the impossible.

This moment really impacted me on so many levels, especially the creative miracle power released through prayer and a fresh revelation that compassion heals. Scripture often says Jesus was moved by compassion, and power and healing would flow. If we want a power upgrade, we need a love upgrade. It touches my heart every time I see God release a miracle. I'm always aware this is not just another miracle for them, it's restoring their very lives!

I don't remember ever not knowing that God was real growing up or ever doubting that He's supernatural, as I've had encounters all my life of God's realness. I've also been aware of the devil's realness and the battle he rages to prevent us from knowing God's goodness. It's with the perspective of years, decades now, that I can look back and say with road-tested confidence that even in the hardest of moments, my King is real, powerful, and has never left my side.

I think all believers have walked real journeys of a mix of valleys and mountaintops. During my life journey, I've discovered that the mountaintops refuel me with determination that if the King and I can do that, then what else can we conquer together next? Every win, big or small, I'm always aware God is my biggest cheerleader and celebrates the wins no one else knows about or sees. There's never been a win that I haven't been aware came from His grace and His constant decrees of truth and promise over me. I'm challenged often to believe in myself as much as God believes in me. I mean, wow, that's a faith-building exercise to think about. God's belief in me has made all the difference.

I live with a daily, eternal purpose before me that never escapes my thinking. One day when I've run my race and I meet my King

Jesus in the throne room of Heaven, I want to look in His eyes and see that sparkle that is reserved just for me and the knowing smile that only a Father and closest of Friend can give. The One who has watched over me and knows the real story behind the story. I live to hear those beautiful, rewarding words, *"Well done, My good and faithful one"* (see Matthew 25:23). I have tears just thinking about this. This future moment drives me, stirs me, and marks everything I do. God knows your story behind the story too, and my prayer is you know Jesus loves you, believes in you, and has a hope and a future for you that is good (see Jeremiah 29:11).

I think we prefer when people "get" us, like us, and champion us; but it's God's opinion of us that matters in eternity. I'm very "eternity aware" in my everyday life. I always have been, I guess. I live with a compelling knowing that life is precious and eternity is near. Consequently, I often ask myself the following questions that help me prioritize what matters most:

- Have I added joy to the Lord today?
- Have I prioritized God in my heart and schedule today?
- Did what really matters, matter most today?
- Am I using my voice to speak life and hope in others?
- What is God saying about this? What is God saying about my next season?
- Was His heart at the forefront of that decision?
- Am I still hungry for more?
- Am I living from what seems logical or have I given space for supernatural solutions?

- Have I allowed unbelief masquerading as wisdom to infiltrate what I'm believing for?
- Have I listened and obeyed the last time God spoke to me?
- Have I taken time today to prioritize my thanks and love to the One I say is first?
- Does the King's decree to me give me radical hope to pursue what others say can't be done?
- Am I loving others well? Have I loved my Friend Jesus well today?
- Is fear influencing my decisions?

In our journey with God there is grace. I sure have learned that, but I've equally discovered that it's the hard, raw questions we ask ourselves when the stuff of life is stripped back in challenging moments that show us what we really believe and whose voice matters most to us.

It's in the *"darkest of valleys"* (Psalm 23:4), that I've discovered the King of kings is the truest of friends, the constant who never changes, the very word of life that sustains, revives and rewrites stories with great victories and redeeming miracles. When I look back at some of my journey, to be honest, I never want to walk through some of those seasons and hard challenges again—yet I also wouldn't wish them away.

I don't believe for a second that pain, sickness, or disaster comes from God, the author of what *"steals, kills, and destroys"* is the devil (John 10:10). But God's presence *with me* as I've walked through "valleys of the shadow of death" and heard His voice and the precious revelation He said to me, is a gift that has made me who I am today. As I look back, it's not the pain I remember, it's the voice of the King's decrees and His tenderness, nearness, and fierceness that scatters the enemy. It's when the enemy and life's obstacles arrogantly say, "You shall not pass"—I just had to have a *Lord of the Rings* reference—that the King's words, "I have made a way for you" become *"alive and active"* (Hebrews 4:12).

It's when I've been at my end and only had God's word and promises to stand on, that I've discovered that this is actually all we ever have. To think any differently is just a mirage. To stand and decree God's word and heart is the most empowering, mountain-shifting, future-shaping, life-giving action we can take. The King's decree when received and released changes everything and expands the borders of our faith. It's from here, the natural is shifted.

I remember a time being in the hospital, when for a season, I needed to regularly receive medication via drip infusion. As my family and I decreed healing and we declared Jesus' blood speaks a better word, we believed for miracle solutions in the middle of circumstances that were trying hard to prophesy fear. The nurse prepared my arm for the drip by cleaning it with an alcohol wipe. As she wiped my arm, *silver* appeared all over my arm! Yes—silver dust appeared everywhere she wiped and wouldn't wipe off as hard as the nurse tried! I saw it, Ben and our daughter saw it, even the nurse saw it as she tried unsuccessfully to "clean" my arm!

What a practical demonstration of the power of our prayers and declarations. Silver in the Bible represents redemption, and I knew in this moment God was extending the borders of my faith, decreeing redemption, and reminding me He would redeem what the enemy had stolen—if God can put a little silver on my arm, He can heal and redeem my health! God was expanding the borders of my faith—the King's decree changes things.

Thank God for my Friend the King who has graciously whispered truths to me and let's be real; sometimes He had to shout until I finally heard! But always, *always* He has been faithful in speaking life and breakthrough when the enemy shouted, "You're not going to get there!" You can insert what "*there*" represents for you in that scenario, because the devil uses the same tactics for everyone. I bet he's told you that you're not going to get "there." Don't listen to him. It's a lie laced in fear to keep you from decreeing God's promises.

I've always *known* God growing up, and I've always "seen" supernatural evidence of a supernatural realm that is bigger than what we currently live in, which compelled me to seek after more. At 3 years of age, after watching the Christmas TV special, *"Little Drummer Boy,"* I cried for days because I wanted to "see Jesus"! The show ends with Jesus being born and I saw His crib, but it never actually shows baby Jesus clearly. My parents say I was inconsolable and they started getting genuinely worried when I wouldn't stop crying, "I want to see Jesus" over and over for days. I do understand my 3-year-old self though—of course I wanted to see Jesus! I still do! I can remember actually hiding in the bathroom of all places, and wailing to see Jesus.

I can also remember what can only be described as demonic attacks, and visions I didn't understand, tormented me with fear when I was young. Nobody needed to tell me demons were real, as I saw or felt them. Thank God, His name is higher and God always pursued my heart—Jesus is greater than *any* demonic fear. I remember clearly being 11 years old and rushed to hospital with a suspected burst appendix. While awaiting emergency surgery, I suddenly awoke in extreme pain and fear in the night and tried to get a nurse's attention. I couldn't get anyone's attention though.

Nobody heard me. I remember being scared for my life and whispering quietly in the dark, "Jesus, I need Your help," and immediately the pain completely disappeared. I realized, God heard me ask for help. These things marked me with God's bigness.

Also in my 11th year, I was nearly blinded in one eye by an ulcer that wouldn't clear up and threatened to cover over my pupil with scar tissue. Seven operations later, each time removing the top layer of skin from my eye, things weren't improving. I was awake for these surgeries, and I remember God's tangible peace coming when I desperately prayed while I was scared in the surgical chair with a scalpel on my eye. I've never forgotten that. I knew God was with me. I had to wear an eye patch for a year to protect my eye from further infection and light and to prevent blindness. So my final year of primary school was spent wearing a black pirate's patch—not the most fun, or *cool* thing to wear when I was already ridiculously shy. And, I wasn't allowed outside for that entire year.

My grandmother, decided she would pick me up for lunch every day and we'd often have sneaky, fun outings at McDonald's or "inside picnics" at her house designed to make me feel special so I didn't have to sit in the classroom alone. Nana amazingly turned bleak into wonderful and I looked forward to lunch that whole year. But the ulcer continued to rage; and despite every medical effort, it was literally bumping up against the barrier where I would be permanently blinded by the scar tissue if it went any further.

We were all praying; I was praying. At the eleventh hour, things changed. It was a great day when my eye specialist said the ulcer was *suddenly* inactive. He said, "You can take that patch off, young lady, and go outside again!" That was a big day, as I knew God had healed me and saved my eyesight.

These things marked me with the revelation, "My God is big!"

For most of my adult life and big chunks of my childhood, I've had varying health challenges, and many times faced impossible odds. Each time I knew that without God doing something, I would be in trouble. In the middle of those very moments, as I cried out to God, so many "suddenlies" took place, and my awareness of God's nearness and "bigness" grew.

At age 19, I was diagnosed with a medically incurable bowel disease that unfortunately caused other complications and life-controlling issues. This impacted my ability to do life normally and make plans free of worry or pain. Complications, reactions to medicines, and failed surgeries only made things worse. It's been a strange journey as I've walked a life of profound healing and health, as well as sickness, and so many wild miracles have happened!

There have been plenty of adventures, despite it all. Family fun and God adventures have taken a high priority in our lives and ministry. I've found that prioritizing fun is warfare! *"The joy of the Lord is your strength"* (Nehemiah 8:10) and His joy is experiential! Thank God it's His joy, and not my joy; because honestly, sometimes my joy runs out, but His joy is reliable and comes from the atmosphere of Heaven!

Joy is essential for everyone. It's especially essential if you are battling a long-term challenge. Joy adds strength, and strength enables perseverance. So joy is warfare! The best kind of warfare some days is to enjoy the Lord! All to say, I thank God for a husband who can make a joke of anything, and adds so much laughter and joy to our lives. Fun, laughter, and joy of the Lord. These are secret ingredients to breakthrough.

I think back to when I was 11 years old, my confidence and self-esteem were in shreds as I was anxious about pretty much everything. I was desperately seeking an answer to how I felt, I just didn't know how to find it yet. I wish I knew then what I know now because what I was about to learn would impact the rest of my life. The King's decree changes everything.

After my 11th year being so difficult with eye challenges, health issues, and facing inner fears, rejections, and demonic torment, I was desperate for real inner peace. Not being allowed outdoors had given me lots of time to study though, and I found a sense of achievement in doing well. I also read book after book about God and the heroes of the Bible, fiction and nonfiction, it didn't matter—I was hungry to learn. I was hungry for the more of God, though I didn't have language for that then. I also know now that God was using this time to speak His heart to me that I was an overcomer and build my confidence. I was really happy when somehow in the middle of all "that," I managed to be awarded Dux of my school, similar to valedictorian. I sensed God's hand on my life, and an inner compelling after God that I would now say was a "call," but I was absolutely desperate for an answer to a question I couldn't yet formulate.

FEAR IS NOT YOUR PROPHET

Honestly, so much changed in my life the day I decided and decreed, "I am not a sick person, and sickness is not who I am, nor will it steal my destiny!" I would say to myself, *I have had health challenges, but I am an overcomer, and God is my Healer, and my destiny will not robbed.* Right then, God breathed truth that ensured that my identity was not in "the stuff" that the enemy was saying about me or throwing at me, but in what my King said about me. Yes, it required faith in what God said, but I was determined not to live my life with fear as my "prophet."

Fear is always looking for a way to prophesy the future—but don't let it speak. Fear is a false prophet and its voice is ringing out like a modern-day Goliath over entire people groups and nations right now. Evict fear and turn up the voice of God. If ever there was a time to amplify the King's decrees of hope and redefine our future based on God's voice, it's now.

Fear is a false prophet and a liar. You will know fear's voice by the inner, fearful reaction that makes you feel as if there is no hope. This reaction is the acid test; it's not from God, and it's not His intention for you. Don't marinate in fear's voice; it will try and take you down a spiral of ever-increasing foreboding darkness. Fear is a spirit, but it's not the Holy Spirit. God is upgrading our awareness of when fear tries to illegally redirect us away from God's heart and purposes in our lives. I know for me, fear has tried to control my life. I've learned that if fear is saying it, I can know God is saying the opposite.

Instead, pray this and say out loud, "Fear, you cannot prophesy to me. I reject your voice in Jesus' name! I may feel fear even now, but I evict, shut down, and ignore your false prophesies. Even if I'm feeling your lingering effects for but a moment, you have no hold on me because you are a liar and nothing you say is truthful about my future. I prophesy peace to my insides. I receive peace from God. I receive God's love that *'drives out fear'* (1 John 4:18). Fear and all its buddies of paralyzing heaviness, dark foreboding thoughts, panic, confusion, distress, hopelessness, shame and misery, and everything birthed from demonic fear, I decree you to take a hike in Jesus' mighty name."

Then, pray to receive a fresh release of hope from God for every circumstance and ask for thoughts that partner with Heaven's promises. Say, "I ask You, Holy Spirit, to infuse every part of me with

Your love, power, and peace. My future is secure in You, Lord." Psalm 28:7 (Amplified Bible) says, *"The Lord is my strength and my [impenetrable] shield."* God's protection of you is impenetrable.

With that in mind, fear is not just trying to prophesy to individuals, but to entire nations. We are on assignment to speak the King's decree and prophesy from Heaven's atmosphere what God is saying. As entire people groups become hysterical with fear, it is even more imperative to ask the question when facing world issues, "Is this fear speaking right now?" Then, speak peace and prophesy God's heart to your nation. Our voice, decreeing truth, will be the determining factor that quells fear's strategies trying to define the future.

Only the King's Decree Defines You

You are not defined by what the enemy has attacked you with, or what the enemy says of you. You are defined only by what *God* says about you. Literally, the King's decree of truth over your life defines who you are.

We need our ears open to receive the King's decree into our lives so we are defined by truth and walk in the authority of the King, which emboldens us to not shrink back as the enemy would have us do. Whatever you have walked through, you are loved, an overcomer, and a child of the King because the King decrees it so! Fear, pain, and doubt will try and prophesy to you. Don't listen! It's a lie.

There is always "stuff" as that's real life. There are always many voices that speak things over our lives, but we get to choose what *voices* we will give influence to. Will we give controlling influence to lies, fear, and dream-limiting voices? Or will we give influence to the King's decree?

Praise Changes the Atmosphere

I've always wanted to be a singer. In reality, though, I'll just say that singing is not my best gift. It's a bit of an inside family joke that I'm going to finally get my "call-up" to worship-lead with Ben and Keely during one of our services. I often joke that in Heaven I'm a worship leader! I even prayed to be a worship leader when I was in my 20s—I really did. Now our daughter, Keely, is a phenomenal worship leader This blesses me and everyone who hears her. My husband, Ben, is also an incredible worship leader who carries breakthrough. I am so truly thankful to have a worshipping family. Their worship at home and in private has revolutionized my life. In truth, I'm a terrible singer, really bad, but I am a passionate worshipper. I know that worship and praise changes the atmosphere and sets us up for miracles.

> *But you are holy, enthroned on the praises of Israel* (Psalm 22:3 CSB).

Ben talks about Psalm 22:3 all the time. God is enthroned on our praise. Worship and praise are forms of declaration that enthrones God over our lives. Worship decrees truth; and the truth is, God is worthy, always! Regardless of what's going on around us or in us, God is worthy of our praise. And it's also true to say that when we don't feel like worshipping, this is the best time to *"Bless the Lord, O my soul"* (Psalm 103:1 NASB) and tell our souls to bless God.

When I genuinely do this, I always find my feelings soon follow and I'm not just saying God is worthy by "faith," I'm saying it with my whole heart and soul. He is worthy, always. Praise, declaration, worship, and decrees shift the atmosphere and enthrone the King over our lives and circumstances.

I also know that if praise enthrones the King and truth, then my words that release doubt, complaints, fear, or distrust enthrone something too. That atmosphere is not what I want to empower in my life or live under. I catch myself sometimes being critical, for instance, and have to reel myself back in.

To live in an atmosphere of faith, miracles, and God's manifest presence, requires seeding an atmosphere of faith, miracles, and God's manifest presence. Our own mouths are empowered to do this. We are empowered as the King's mouthpiece. As for me, I can't afford to *not* live in this atmosphere.

You Are the King's Mouthpiece

We are empowered to be the King's mouthpiece on earth. We have the full authority of the King to speak forth God's promises and affect change in our lives as much as in our generation. We are called in Job 22:28 (NASB) to *"decree a thing and it will be established for you"* with our voices.

Yes, our voices, our prayers, our faith, our decrees, and our mouths shall decree a thing and we will see it established in the season in which we live. No one else is called to establish the Kingdom in our generation, than we who are alive right now. We are called to carry God's authority and speak forth God-change. If *we* don't speak, "Come out of the grave" to our prophetic Lazarus circumstances and nations, who will? Lazarus would have stayed in the grave had Jesus not decreed, *"Come forth!"* (John 11:43 NASB).

What if our sphere of influence, in our lives and journeys, is awaiting our decree of "Come forth"? What never-seen-before breakthroughs are on the other side of our voice decreeing, "Dry bones live again" (Ezekiel 37)? What miracles of comeback and turnaround will bow as we say, "My King says something different"? If ever there was a season, if ever there was an hour for our voices to partner with Heaven and speak, it's now, my friend.

The authority on our decrees has been bought by the blood of Jesus. Use it. Speak life. Speak hope. Just speak. Jesus paid for us to be free, not intimidated.

Intimidation has a sneaky way of keeping your reach small, contained, and joyless. Break free, take the muzzle off in the spirit, and unleash the uniqueness you carry. Your voice, your story, your faith becomes a mouthpiece and catalyst of change.

UNEXPECTED ARMY

Something unexpected happened along the way of my journey. I think it's probably been the same for many of you. I realized I am a sign and wonder of God's goodness. I realized I am a weapon in God's hand. I realized my mouth, words, and decrees are not just powerful, but crucial and *must* be released. The same is true for you, friend.

The King's decree from *your* mouth is changing history one decree at a time, one faith-filled action at a time. There's an unexpected army arising that the world didn't see coming. A people who have been forged in the fire, but now carry fire. Their mouths release consuming fire and are poised to light revival fires with their decrees. Every decree these fiery ones release establishes greater glory and redeems stories in their own lives and nations.

This new breed arising is not afraid of their journeys; they are not hiding from them, and are not held back by them. Instead, they are empowered by God's truth that what the enemy meant for harm, God intends for good (read Genesis 50:20). There are times in all our lives when, if we are honest, we feel vulnerable, inadequate, broken, or scared; but that's when we most need to listen to the King's voice and declare boldly with Him, *"Let the weak say, 'I am strong!'"* (Joel 3:10 NKJV).

There is nothing as powerful as the King's decree in our lives. Nothing! What the King says is the final, undisputed word. Therefore, silence untruths and listen to the word of God. Our future is determined by what God says, not our past struggles, failures, fears, and most definitely not what the enemy says. As His mouthpiece, God is invested in our heart health, *"For out of the abundance of the heart his* [the] *mouth speaks"* (Luke 6:45 NKJV).

We've all had journeys of valleys and mountains, and the King says to us, *"after your brief suffering, the God of all loving grace, who has called you to share in his eternal glory in Christ, will personally and powerfully restore you and make you stronger than ever. Yes, he will set you firmly in place and build you up"* (1 Peter 5:10 TPT). Did you get that? Where there has been suffering, hurts, and pain, God promises He will personally and powerfully restore and build you up, until you are stronger than before!

As His mouthpiece on the earth, God is personally and powerfully invested in our hearts. My prayer is: "Heal our hearts, Lord, so our mouths speak words that restore, heal, build up, and truly convey the heart of our King."

And so—when I remember that lady I shared about who looked six months pregnant from inflammation and was healed before our eyes saying, "I don't know if you can understand," this is why it stirred such compassion in me. I immediately wept as the compassion of God came on me, and I remembered time and time again when I faced physical pain, fears, an uncertain future, and was in desperate need for supernatural breakthrough. God still turns things around.

I take every one of these testimonies and life lessons and use them to urge me on to decree the King's heart over others. Those words resonated and activated such deep compassion in me for this lady to get her life back that day. Compassion still drives me to partner with the King's decree and simple mandate to restore people's lives. It's the same for nations. The King is speaking life in the face of destruction, and we are called as His mouthpieces to decree the same.

THE KING'S DECREE FOR YOU

"I formed you in your mother's womb. I have always been with you, I have never left you. I know you deeply and I know how to speak to you in your language. You can be confident in this, YOU hear My voice. You know My voice, My child. Keep leaning in to listen, keep talking to Me, there are amazing conversations ahead of us. My heart delights every time we talk."
—THE KING

MY PRAYER FOR YOU

You are who God says you are, and I prophesy over you even now that every lie from the pit of hell that has come to squash you, steal your hope, minimize your influence, or keep you trapped in soul-destroying chains is broken in Jesus' name. Where you have been weak, I say you are strong. I bless you with new courage and tell any assignment of fear that has come against you, tormented, or hindered you, to be broken in Jesus' name. I decree influence and chain-breaking fire on your voice, mighty one. Your voice carries Heaven's authority, and I pray greater confidence and rising hope within you. You are a blessing right where God has placed you, and I ask for open doors and favor. May you encounter God in fresh, tangible, and powerful ways today. In Jesus' name, amen.

DECREE

- Fear is not my prophet—my future is determined by what God says.
- I am not defined by the battles and circumstances I have faced, but by who God says I am.
- I am the King's mouthpiece on earth; my voice is needed.
- I have full authority to speak forth God's promises and to affect change in my generation.
- My community is blessed by my voice.
- My mouth, my words, and my decrees are not just powerful, they are crucial.

Chapter 3

"ASK ME!"

Ask me and I will tell you remarkable secrets
you do not know about things to come.
—Jeremiah 33:3 NLT

Just like I'd hear you if you were in my room talking, I suddenly heard an audible, clear, loud voice speak to me. Just two words, but they have impacted my life ever since. I was alone in my bedroom, only 12 years old, and nothing like that had ever happened before, yet I instantly knew God was speaking to me. I thought surely the whole house must have heard as it was *that* loud, or maybe the whole suburb had heard an unusual thunder.

His voice was deep, tender, and kind, and yet commanding. I inherently knew to listen, as everything in my body was a little unnerved and suddenly alert. I had been particularly anxious that morning, feeling ridiculously stressed and worried about my life and going to high school. Shyness had become quite debilitating; and being around people or anything unfamiliar filled me with fear that made me feel sick. I was fearful of the unknown, and sadly even fearful of the known, as life had already shown me it wasn't always kind. I'd retreated into myself to find peace, but even there I only found uncertainties and more fears.

Memories troubled me of feeling alone at school and never quite fitting in. I wondered what was wrong with me. Then I discovered one day that some "friends" had literally paid off other kids to not talk to me, which added to my distrust of people and thoughts that I wasn't good enough. Yes, money was actually exchanged to bribe kids not to be my friend! Feeling ostracized left a loud question in my heart that became an accusation, "There's something wrong with me."

Add to this mix was the fact that I was very spiritually aware, and many of my interactions with the spirit realm had been dark and scared me. I absolutely knew God was real and I had a real relationship with Him. There was a strange blend of experiences going on as I dreamed of stadiums, preaching, healing people, and impacting the nations. While at the same time I was so scared I'd wrap myself up in blankets at the end of my parents' bed trying to hide from supernatural encounters I didn't understand.

I'm the eldest of all my cousins and sisters, and as a child when we were all at Nana's house, I'd write sermons and make all the other kids sit in chairs facing me while I preached! I'm not sure if they enjoyed that much, but hey, I planted my first church in my nana's spare bedroom!

The dark, demonic stuff I saw and experienced, though, convinced me that something terrible could happen at any time and I thought I had little or no power to stop it, which added to my constant fear. I had an amazing Christian upbringing, so none of these things made me doubt God was real, but I was never fully at peace or comfortable in my own skin. I lived every day in torment that was very real and inescapable. Fear started infusing everything and detrimentally affecting my decisions. I speak to so many who have faced similar issues growing up, or even still are. The good news is, there's an answer.

"ASK ME" DAY CHANGED EVERYTHING

Going to high school filled me with dread. I never felt at peace and was convinced something terrible would happen to me. Through no fault of my family, I felt like nobody understood or could help, which resulted in thinking my life would always be miserable. I was panicked wondering where I could go for help. Who could help? Who could I ask? I felt alone. I felt without hope. It was into this space that suddenly God spoke. I heard only two words but they changed everything!

His voice had a sound I'll never forget. I now know why the Bible says, *"His voice was like the sound of many waters"* (Ezekiel 43:2; Revelation 1:15, 14:2 NKJV). The only sound since then that vaguely reminds me of how God sounded that day was in revival. That sound when revival is stirring in the room…it's more of a feeling even than a sound, but it resonates, it stirs, it thunders, it awakens. There is a sound in revival that ruins you for the normal; it echoes in your spirit and marks you. God's voice did the same. It still echoes in me all these years later. God's voice resonated in every cell of my body as He said, "Ask Me!"

I immediately understood that if God was saying something I had better listen and do what He was saying. So I timidly said,

"Okay God, I'm asking." I don't think I knew what I was asking for, and I certainly didn't expect what happened next.

Suddenly I felt a warm, thick, honey-like substance start pouring down over me from my head first, and slowly dripping down my entire body—not an inch of me was left untouched. That's the only way I can describe it. Thick, weighty honey with a comforting warmth to it. As this substance continued to drip down my entire body it literally removed fear! I could feel it happening. A tangible peace was taking over until it soaked every part of me!

I know I had tears, but they were tears of relief. I had *never* felt such peace. All my anxious thoughts suddenly left. I felt different. I felt God's power. I felt His tenderness. I felt His safety. I knew He sought me out personally and was in my room with me that morning, not far away, but right there answering a little girl's cry. God had seen me and God had spoken to me. It was the deepest, most total peace and stillness I had ever felt. The honey-like warmth infused me with a knowing; I was protected, safe, loved, and personally cared for by God.

"Ask Me"—those two words have stayed with me every single day since. It was simple. But it was life changing. How could just two words convey so much? I "knew" God, who spoke these words was good, my Father, and delighted in me. Just knowing that made me cry. My Father in Heaven adored me. I felt it in His voice. You too have the same Father.

The answer to every question, fear, or concern I could ever have was contained in those powerful words, "Ask Me." The King of kings and Lord of lords in one moment spoke hope and love into me that marked every day from then.

No matter what life can throw at us, no matter what lies the devil wants to convince us of, no matter what torment we are going through, there is always hope. God Himself is the answer, the solution, and the redeemer of any story we find ourselves in the middle of. And He is still decreeing into each of our stories, "Ask Me." Even as a 12-year-old, I knew this was the answer I was looking for, this was eternal truth. This voice commanded darkness to flee and it obeyed. I knew instantly *this* voice belonged to the God who is bigger, higher, greater; and nothing, *no thing* was more powerful than Him!

All my circumstances didn't immediately shift and change, as there was a process I had to walk out as I grew in truth, as all of us need to do. But I know God changed the course of my life that day and a divine hunger was imparted to know not just His voice, but the God behind the words that could evict fear and command peace to the storms.

Hearing God puts a childlike simplicity of trust in our hearts knowing that nothing, *nothing* is outside of God's reach. I wanted, no, needed, to know more about that God. His words thundered from Heaven right into my bedroom and His voice decreed words that changed things. *Wow,* I remember thinking, *His voice is powerful! His voice thunders! Why had I never known before how powerful His voice was?! And all I had to do was ask!* That day, the "Ask Me" day, truly changed everything. My God was powerful. My God talked. My God had words that scared fear. And His words brought change.

Those two words, "Ask Me," are being said to entire nations right now. God is saying, "Ask Me" to politicians, media makers, mums and dads, entrepreneurs, the world's activists and future catalysts, influencers and celebrities, students and teachers, lawmakers and lawbreakers, people in every culture with every worldview, those who sit up at night worrying about wars, those who worry about the climate, relationship issues, how to pay the bills, and those feeling alone, scared and looking for answers. God is shouting over each person worldwide, "ASK ME!"

Within the question the answer is found. God doesn't say, "Ask Me," and not have a solution. God Himself is the answer to the questions and has *"remarkable secrets"* (Jeremiah 33:3) to share filled with profound solutions when He's asked.

BE STILL AND KNOW

On the back wall of my childhood church was a verse my grandfather chose, one that I looked at every week growing up in The Salvation Army: *"Be still, and know that I am God"* (Psalm 46:10). This verse was always special, but after the "Ask Me" day, it became more real than real as I suddenly understood the power of the Author who wrote those words.

It wasn't the end of the Goliaths I faced, but it was the end of feeling alone and without hope, and the beginning of my love affair with the Author of the universe who speaks things and "stuff" changes! The King's decree is the ultimate chain-breaking weapon of transformation and God-change on the earth. And He invites us to ask Him for secrets we don't know, solutions and supernatural interventions that evict the enemy's plans. God wants us to ask Him what He thinks, and then gives us the authority to speak on His behalf and partner with Him decreeing with the same power He carries!

Nothing God ever says contradicts or disagrees with His written Word. Yes, of course read and know the Bible, friend. Can I say that again—*read and know the Bible.* God will never violate Scripture. Sometimes, however, God will say things that disrupt our interpretation or limited understanding of the Bible. God is bigger than our limitations we put on Him, and He likes to show us that!

You're Protected

If you've never really soaked in Psalm 91, let the words speak to your season and the doors God is opening for you. You are protected wherever you go, and He will answer and be your glorious Hero as you step into the things He is talking to you about.

I love these selected verses from Psalm 91:

> *He will rescue you from every hidden trap of the enemy, and he will protect you from false accusation and any deadly curse.*
>
> *His massive arms are wrapped around you, protecting you. You can run under his covering of majesty and hide. His arms of faithfulness are a shield keeping you from harm.*
>
> *You will never worry about an attack of demonic forces at night nor have to fear a spirit of darkness coming against you.*
>
> *Don't fear a thing! Whether by night or by day, demonic danger will not trouble you, nor will the powers of evil launched against you.*
>
> *God sends angels with special orders to protect you wherever you go, defending you from all harm.*
>
> *I will answer your cry for help every time you pray, and you will find and feel my presence even in your time of pressure and trouble. I will be your glorious hero and give you a feast.* (Psalm 91:3-6,11,15 TPT).

And so, God says to us, "Ask Me." Whatever is going on, whatever we are facing, nothing, *no thing*, is more powerful than God and His decree. Fear itself is scared of the King's decree and of those who know their authority in God to speak!

You may not have had a journey like mine, but you no doubt relate to feeling overwhelmed by, and fearful of, the unknown at times. Or being in a pressured situation that needs breakthrough. Or feeling alone and like no one truly understands what has been going on as you've battled to walk in the fullness of your promises. I tell you friend, God does *not* author fear, destruction, harm or confusion. He does however author redeeming stories of miraculous solutions. God is restoring, rewriting, and reworking all the details, small and big, to bring new beginnings of hope to the feasting table of your heart. He promises that He Himself will be "your glorious hero."

The words "Ask Me" are so refreshingly simple they've influenced how I pray ever since. Childlike trust is the key to asking God and decreeing, not a theological degree! The worst of religion wants to make prayer so complicated and arduous that we avoid it. But it's meant to be simple, refreshing, and easy.

So here's my simple, everyday, real-person "theology of asking God":

1. Ask Him!

2. Speak out what He says.

3. Do what He says.

Do this, and "stuff" changes.

End of theology lesson.

Asking is mentioned throughout Scripture. God says, "Ask Me" because it is simple. Check out these Bible verses:

> ***Ask me*** *and I will tell you remarkable secrets you do not know about things to come* (Jeremiah 33:3 NLT).

> ***Ask me,*** *and I will make the nations your inheritance, the ends of the earth your possession* (Psalm 2:8).

> ***Ask*** *and it will be given to you; seek and you will find; knock and the door will be opened to you* (Matthew 7:7).

> *And I will do whatever you* ***ask*** *in my name, so that the Father may be glorified in the Son* (John 14:13).

> *And all things you* ***ask*** *in prayer, believing, you will receive* (Matthew 21:22 NASB).

> *So I say to you,* ***ask,*** *and it will be given to you; seek, and you will find; knock, and it will be opened to you. For everyone who* ***asks***, *receives; and he who seeks, finds; and to him who knocks, it will be opened* (Luke 11:9-10 NASB).

> *But if any of you lacks wisdom, let him* ***ask*** *of God...* (James 1:5 NASB).

> *Until now you have not asked for anything in my name.* ***Ask*** *and you will receive, and your joy will be complete* (John 16:24).

> *At Gibeon the Lord appeared to Solomon during the night in a dream, and God said, "****Ask*** *for whatever you want me to give you"* (1 Kings 3:5).

> *If imperfect parents know how to lovingly take care of their children and give them what they need, how much more will the perfect heavenly Father give the Holy Spirit's fullness when his children* ***ask*** *him* (Luke 11:13 TPT).

*Just make sure you **ask** empowered by confident faith without doubting that you will receive. For the ambivalent person believes one minute and doubts the next. Being undecided makes you become like the rough seas driven and tossed by the wind. You're up one minute and tossed down the next. When you are half-hearted and wavering it leaves you unstable. Can you really expect to receive anything from the Lord when you're in that condition?* (James 1:6-8 TPT)

*If you, imperfect as you are, know how to lovingly take care of your children and give them what's best, how much more ready is your heavenly Father to give wonderful gifts to those who **ask** him?* (Matthew 7:11 TPT)

And read this beautiful promise from God about prayer and asking:

*Don't be pulled in different directions or worried about a thing. Be saturated in prayer throughout each day, **offering your faith-filled requests** before God with overflowing gratitude. Tell him every detail of your life, then God's wonderful peace that transcends human understanding, will make the answers known to you through Jesus Christ* (Philippians 4:6-7 TPT).

There are more examples than these in the Bible, but that's enough to highlight that God wanted it known and is still saying today, "Ask Me." He made it simple on purpose. There are so many things in the Kingdom that require our partnership before we receive, and *asking is the first step.*

I've noticed in the years since I've actively and purposefully been asking for "more," there is observably more. I've seen more miracles, had more encounters, more healings happen when praying for people, and more manifestations of God's glory realm. Basically, since asking for more, I've had more! I want to see much more, so I continue to ask, step out, and decree more.

Our Love of God Compels Us to Ask for More

I'll never forget in Fiji praying for a lady who was blind; her daughter was next to her. I simply prayed and asked for her to see as we've been talking about. She still couldn't see when I checked, so I prayed again. This time she nodded yes. She said it so matter of factly that I asked the daughter to ask her mother again. After she spoke with her mother, I asked, "You mean she can see now?!" The daughter answered, "Yes, she can see!" Praise God, I jumped in the air, yelled and laughed! I watched the lady walk herself back to her seat without her daughter needing to guide her. I thought, *Wow, God, that woman's entire life has been changed! I want to see more of that!* This, and other miracles, compel me to ask God for more. May we ask for more, so we can walk in more.

Some time ago, a man I knew and trusted walked up to me and gave me a word that wasn't a comfortable word to hear, and yet it was said in kindness and I knew it was the Lord speaking gently to me. The man said to me, "Jodie, you have great faith, you believe in the God of the impossible and asking Him for great things. You have faith for the miraculous and supernatural when you ask, *but* God says, you're not asking Him."

Ouch. What God said through that man stopped me in my tracks. It sort of hurt. But actually it hit my heart and I didn't hear any judgment. I heard the kindness of my God who all those years before had spoken and said, "Ask Me." I realized in a moment, I had stopped deliberately pressing in as much and extending my faith to believe for more than I had before. I had stopped asking for expansion of my faith, extension of my ability to believe, to see more than I had ever seen before. I realized I'd stopped speaking out big requests and asking God for the impossible in some areas of my life. It wasn't that I didn't believe, I had just stopped actively and purposefully *asking*. It was a kind wake-up call.

God still says, "Ask Me."

Why? Because He answers our faith to ask. The King loves friendship and heart connection. He desires us to ask.

The key to divine revelation and more in the glory realm, is to *ask!* I wonder how much more we could live in if we actively, persistently, and deliberately asked for more? God's saying to us, "Ask Me." What have we stopped asking the Lord for? Are there places we can reconnect and simply start the conversation again—and ask the King who answers?

THE KING'S DECREE FOR YOU

"I have remarkable things to tell you that you do not know. I am excited to share My secrets with you. Ask Me. Ask Me for what you need. Ask Me to share My heart with you. Ask Me for My secrets. There is no end to what I will share with you."
—THE KING

MY PRAYER FOR YOU

I bless your ears to hear God's voice with fresh clarity and new ease. I call in peace to the storms, and ask for excitement as you think of what God is leading you into. These are the days you are made for and this season is your most fruitful. You are celebrated and loved and I ask for a fresh revelation of how God sees you. I pray redemptive solutions to every area in your life. As you pray, I speak new childlike joy, awe and wonder, and a grace for deeper connection and vulnerable friendship with King Jesus. In Jesus' name. Amen.

DECREE

- I am entering remarkable days, and I am hungry for more of God.
- I am expectant in Your presence, Lord, to hear Your voice speak fresh revelation and wisdom.
- Nothing can stop what God is orchestrating for me.
- You are a good Father and so I come boldly as a child and simply ask.

Chapter 4

THE LAZARUS ANOINTING

*Our friend Lazarus has fallen asleep; but I
am going there to wake him up.*
—JOHN 11:11

Every challenge, every obstacle, every learning curve, every battle, every private win—all of it, the highs and the lows, and the everyday faithfulness and struggles you fought through that no one else saw, have prepared you for the crescendo of victories you're about to win. This has certainly been the case for me.

Those battles you've won in private, yes even those battles that threatened to destroy you, will become the breakthroughs celebrated in public. However, this time, you have authority to take others with you into breakthrough. There's a harvest of breakthroughs behind your courage. That's why it's been so hard. The enemy is not just scared of your breakthrough, he's afraid of all the other breakthroughs about to break open as you come back even stronger!

Lazarus-style comeback stories are going to become increasingly commonplace as the King breathes resurrection life over promises that have been latent, delayed, or fought hard against. God is restoring your story, taking what the enemy meant for harm and turning it for good. And your voice is part of this process.

WHEN A KING DECREES

An earthly king doesn't just talk about circumstances, he commands and makes declarations that bring solutions and change. A king's decree is the final say. A king's decree carries the full weight of his authority and power to back it up.

So it goes without saying that when *the* King of kings decrees breakthrough and swift change, there is no power in Heaven or on earth that can stand in the way of what God has decreed. His decree releases life-shifting, chain-breaking, nation-shaking power. God is looking for a people who when faced with challenges, bring out their swords, and decree God's word into the earth.

> Jesus said to him, "What do you mean 'if'? **If you are able to believe, all things are possible** to the believer" (Mark 9:23 TPT).

Praying like this shifts circumstances. Heaven is not running out of resurrection power or creative solutions earmarked for any obstacle we bump into. I've seen God show up when I thought all hope was lost for me. He is doing the same all around the earth right now where a new breed of warrior is arising who knows how to declare on behalf of the King. Knowing this authority to partner with the throne room and speak to dead places in our lives is foundational to seeing Lazarus-style turnarounds and miracles (Mark 16:17-20).

It's Comeback Time

Where there's been a theme of attack that has come against you, it's the sure sign that you're called to walk in authority in this area and lead others to the same breakthrough. As I write this I just checked the time and it's 11:11 a.m. A reminder to me of John 11:11 and the power of resurrection life and the Lazarus anointing to bring people's destiny back to life. The God of Lazarus sparks faith that dead places can live again. Over and over in my life God has given kind, and pretty specific, miracles to emphasize impossible is only impossible when we consider it so.

Bill Johnson says, "We know our minds have been renewed when the impossible seems logical." This quote stirs faith in me. God wants to use us to do the impossible, and it begins with renewing our thinking and aligning our declarations with upgraded faith.

I often pray, "God, expand what I am prepared to believe You for. Show me more than I've seen before. Teach me *how* to trust You for what I haven't experienced yet, and release notable miracles that will turn a generation to Your heart. May impossible never be a roadblock to me when You speak, God, but a challenge to increase my faith."

God has been highlighting John 11:11 to me for what seems forever now. As I look back it's been a theme, a kiss from Heaven, and very definitely something that God has been growing a strength to not just recognize God is saying this, but recognize God is releasing this as an authority to walk in. The Lazarus anointing for comeback is for where the enemy has tried to squash, contain, hinder, and kill what God is doing. Yes, real resurrections are happening increasingly worldwide in certain ministries and situations—as the resurrection power of Jesus has paid for everything that the devil has tried to kill off.

What the enemy has thrown at you will not succeed in its intention, as God is releasing new strategies, new breakthroughs, and new power to override all that has come against you. It is essential we speak life, though, especially when the enemy is speaking destruction. Too often because the enemy's voice is loud, we can be found agreeing with what the enemy is saying instead of partnering with God. The Lazarus anointing requires faith as it is illogical without God's power to speak life to dead places in our lives.

What God shows us as revelation in one season, is our key to promise in another. Take note when God is confirming and highlighting a revelation to you. Decreeing "live again" is the essence of revival. Over the years, it seemed everywhere we turned God was growing faith in us for the impossible.

OUR CAR

Ben was finishing Bible College many years ago now, and to cut a long story short, our car died. And when I say died, I mean died! Living on minimal income, we had fixed the car a thousand times before just to keep it on the road; but this time, it was beyond repair. The cost of repair was extensively more than the car was worth. More to the point, we also didn't have the money to buy another car.

As we often did, we stopped and prayed as a family. Keely, who was around 6 years old at the time, announced, "God said John 11." We read John 11 and knew what God was saying, "Resurrection life for Lazarus." We also had ministry friends who used to joke about calling their car "Lazarus," as it had come back from the dead so many times! But honestly, Ben nor I could imagine our car coming back from the dead this time. We knew we needed a car, but didn't have a way to sort out the problem. We just prayed and asked God for a John 11 miracle, with trust that God would work something out, quickly we hoped, but no idea what would unfold.

Ben's friend owned a car dealership and he offered to tow our car to his lot and look at it to give us an honest opinion. I remember working at church one day soon after and getting a phone call from Ben to come outside quickly. It sounded so urgent, I rushed outside. To my utter amazement, I walked out the front door of the church and there was Ben driving our "dead" car! I had to look twice, okay three times, because I couldn't believe what I saw! It was even shining!

The owner of the car dealership had secretly decided to repair our car from top to bottom as a gift to us. Literally thousands and thousands of dollars of repairs was done—from big things like the timing belt, steering, alternator, and the air conditioner to little things like even painting the tires and replacing a light inside the car that had never worked. Every single broken thing was fixed or replaced. And here it was in front of our eyes! This man even detailed the car and gave us a $150 voucher to dinner at his favorite restaurant to bless us! I cried. Ben cried. We all cried. Wow God!

I couldn't believe it! God brought our car back from the dead! God used that car to bless us and to solidify a truth in our hearts—God *is* the God of Lazarus even today. And our 6-year-old had heard God clearly!

FORECLOSURE

God used our house some years later to reemphasize the same point. Again, in a hard season—let's be real, who hasn't been there—with flared health challenges again that prevented "ministry work" and consequential financial issues, we found ourselves unable to keep up with our home's mortgage payments. We had used every "grace" option available to us. The bank sent the official notice of foreclosure. We tried everything, as you can imagine—talking to banks and getting extensions on every bill, food parcels; praying and believing for healing, breakthrough and this "attack on every side" to stop.

In the middle of fighting serious health issues, the idea of losing our home was upsetting. And all this was happening after an angel came and stood on the end of our bed and commissioned us into Pour It Out Ministries. The irony of ministry behind the scenes is sometimes, well, ironic. Let me tell you, everyone faces battles, especially when they are taking new ground, but there is grace to take every promise God has spoken, even when everything looks the opposite.

We were praying, believing, and decreeing the God of Lazarus would come show Himself strong. The prospect of losing our home made my heart sick. I knew we'd be okay, but knowing the story of the miraculous way we got the house in the first place, personally I struggled with the disappointment of the loss.

Miraculously my health began improving, and we went to Fiji to minister as part of fifty days of revival. What a wild, glorious, fiery time of miracles and revival broke out. I remember Ben praying out loud with us as we took off on the airplane, "God, we give You our house, and we trust You." I said it too and I meant it, and familiar peace comforted me. God's provision didn't end just because I didn't understand the current predicament. I prophesied John 11:11 many times in Fiji; and again we felt him saying, "I am the God of Lazarus."

On our return to Australia from the Fiji revival, I was ready to pack up our home reluctantly, and find a new place to live. Real life has strange contradictions sometimes. By some crazy miracle, though, the lady processing our foreclosure had "forgotten" to process our file and had lost it! After months and months of drawn-out failed negotiations and the final decision that the bank was foreclosing, in a moment, the bank decided to reverse its decision and allow us to keep the home! It was that quick, that simple—and astounding!

After this, we immediately rented out our house, and our little family went on the road in outback Australia ministering and releasing revival in every town and city we went through. We prophesied resurrection power all over Australia from tiny town to major city. God was showing us, teaching us, and growing in us that His resurrection power is for nations.

THE PINEAPPLE REVIVAL— CALLING FORTH LIFE

We had prophesied revival all over Australia; and so when we planted Pour It Out Church on the Sunshine Coast of Australia, again we decreed the God of Lazarus, awakening a people to walk in the fullness of all God had promised. We burned with a passion for the nation of Australia to see a nation-shifting revival. What God had done over and over in our lives, we decreed He would do in our nation. It was the greatest of joys and honors when revival broke out and we hosted the Pineapple Revival, as it became known.

During the journey of planting a church we grew a lot when facing the inner challenges, heartaches, and joys of pioneering something from nothing. Going from just the three of us, to fifty people to three and a half years later revival breaking out with more than 20,000 people from all around the world coming, it was amazing. The revival continued for more than eighteen months night after night. Multiple thousands upon thousands of people watched online, and so many times we had to rely upon the God of Lazarus. Speaking forth life to dead places is essentially the definition of what revival is! You can't have revival, personal or corporate, unless you know your voice has authority to decree life to dead things.

There were many times during the revival when finances, people, circumstances, or the devil said this can't go any further. For example, the very first week required believing for four times increase of finances to cover the expenses of a building large enough for the sudden number of hungry people coming from all over. After week one, to continue we urgently needed to find a different building in 48 hours to keep going. Despite a desperate search, we couldn't find a building. People were already arriving from all over Australia. We had no idea how they were even finding out about it.

We were determined that revival wouldn't end just because, *"there was no room for them in the inn"* (Luke 2:7 NKJV). This is how we ended up at a pub in Aussie World, a tourism theme park and pub that amazingly opened its doors to us. Our incredible team got us moved and set up on the same day in an auditorium out the back of a famous Aussie pub. And the people just kept coming from everywhere, night after night after night.

There were daily impossible situations to solve and believe for as you can imagine—including logistical and practical elements— as the revival suddenly grew from fifty people once a week to multiple hundreds of different people every single night. We were in a regional center where people were traveling to from all across the nation, and nations! We thank God He grew us in the private battles, preparing us for the battles ahead.

Again we had to move buildings quickly. When hundreds were coming every night from all around the world, some driving five days to be in God's presence, desperate for a miracle, let me tell you, we feel the weight of stewarding well what God was so graciously pouring out. We had 24 hours to find another building. But God. We and our team were praying and believing for impossible to be made possible.

ANOTHER SUDDENLY MIRACLE

And yes, another *suddenly* miracle happened. God led us to another tourist attraction, The Big Pineapple, a pineapple farm with a 40-foot pineapple at the front and an old events center in the back. It had gone into receivership years before, so it wasn't in good condition when we first saw it. It was empty though, which was a huge plus. But my heart sank when I saw that it needed a *lot* of "love." We were unsure if we should take it as we only had 24 hours to get it ready for all the people who were now coming from various nations worldwide. Lives were being changed every single night. It was beyond life changing—the love of God and level of weighty glory was something none of us had ever felt before. There was electricity in the room, and God Himself was drawing people in.

A few years earlier, Ben and I had received a word from Patricia King, a well-respected apostolic and prophetic minister, when she randomly pointed at us in a meeting and said, "Toot, toot! The glory train is coming to your house!" *Great,* we thought, *and amen!* Little did we know the significance of those words.

As we stood in an empty, old tourism building known as the famous Big Pineapple, we thought, *Is this really it, the place to house this revival?* As The Big Pineapple was still a working tourist attraction, there was a scenic train that continued to operate on the property. As we stood there asking the question of God, "Is this *really* the place you have for us to keep revival going?" Suddenly we heard, "TOOT TOOOOOOOOT!" It was like a modern-day prophetic shofar trumpeting out. We both laughed and said to the manager, "We'll take it!"

That same day, our incredible team with the help of many willing and serving people moved "revival" into a new home. Together, we incredibly made what looked forgotten into a place that was warm and inviting. And the people kept coming! Literally tens of thousands of people encountered God in *that Pineapple!* What a glorious, miraculous, mind-blowing season of revival that became affectionately known as The Pineapple Revival! To think it all could have ended many times over if God had not shown us that He is still making the impossible possible.

Years later, the local newspaper on the Sunshine Coast of Australia ran a story on The Big Pineapple. The front-page headline read, "REVIVAL AT THE BIG PINEAPPLE." Well, I guess "they" caught on! A $150 million dollar redevelopment had been approved to revive The Pineapple to its former glory, and breathe new economic life to the region. What happened in the spirit, then happened in the natural. God's revival power is evidenced in more ways than one. Incidentally, the same thing happened to the pub at Aussie World after we left, they also approved a multimillion dollar makeover. Revival breathes fresh life.

The Pineapple Revival did the same for people's lives as it did for the buildings, fresh life was stirred. Night after night we watched as bodies were healed, hearts came alive, hope was restored, miracles happened, souls were saved, and people authentically fell in love with Jesus. There was such a powerful manifestation, a tangible present-presence of God, that it was impossible to be there and not be marked by the contagious fire for God. All who were part of revival, for just a few nights or for months on end, will never forget the raw hunger and passion after God that was stirred.

Night after night we saw little children, as young as 3, lying on the ground after prayer, unable to move under the power of God for over an hour—this wrecks you for the ordinary. These kids became so on fire for God that they became our prayer team. Adults were constantly overcome by the presence of God as kids and youth prayed for them. One of my favorite sermons during this time came from a 3-year-old boy who brought his Bible to church and put it down next to us. He thought that was how people got to *have* the microphone!

Well, we gave him the mic and his sermon has echoed in my spirit ever since. He stood and yelled with power, "ARRRRRE YOOOOU READYYY!?" Let me tell you, the glory fell. God had spoken through a 3-year-old.

Are *you* ready? The King is coming!

It was not uncommon that joy would break out for hours as God restored hope that the nation could be won for Jesus. There were many nights when the crowd would spontaneously worship for what seemed like forever as God healed people often without anyone praying for them. I remember a soldier who had a long-term shoulder injury from military service and was constantly in pain. His wife told us how he wept when he was healed in worship spontaneously.

Entire families were restored, people who had known God for decades reported encountering God tangibly in a way they never had before, and this activated people to share God's love with others. Suddenly people felt compelled to evangelize their world. God became real, more real than real. It was impossible to be part of this and not fall in love with Jesus the King, and be imparted with a bold faith that God knows how to win a nation.

How grateful I am that God taught us and showed us that impossible isn't the final word, only the King's decree is the final say. I can tell you this, it's a John 11:11 season of awakening people, cities, and nations, and calling forth promises back from the grave. Our voice is designed to call forth Lazarus-style comebacks because we need resurrection working power in every area of our lives.

> *...Our friend, Lazarus has fallen asleep, but I am going there to wake him up* (John 11:11).

PERSPECTIVE SHIFT IS IMPORTANT

When Jesus shows up and speaks to "Lazarus circumstances," people wake up! We can deliberately purpose *our* voice to show up and speak the same faith declarations. Our words awaken divine purpose and evict the enemy's interference in whatever circumstance we aim our faith at.

Jesus notably only refers to the situation of Lazarus in the grave as in need of *waking up*. What a profound perspective shift! It's important we see our challenges through the perspective of Heaven. Yes, they are real challenges. Yes, we need real solutions. And yes, we have the God who specializes in divine comebacks and releasing life where the enemy has ravaged.

Impossible is not a roadblock for a miracle, it's the ingredient of the best Lazarus-comeback miracles. Give greater influence to God's voice, rather than the voice that wants to keep people's lives stuck in grave clothes.

What the enemy means for harm, God turns for good. New authority is on you where you have fought personal battles to now release others into the same breakthroughs. It's been hard because the enemy is scared of not just *your* breakthrough, but the break-through of many others unleashed in your victory. Keep going, friend. You are breaking through.

> *You* [the enemy] *intended to harm me, but God intended it for good to accomplish what is now being done, the saving of many lives* (Genesis 50:20).

What God has grown in us is for us, but it's also for others. For instance, God did not send harm, but as I walked through *my* challenges, He grew a fire in me to see the God of Lazarus show up in healing, creative solutions, financial situations, and more importantly to decree revival to a region and a nation.

Truly, what the enemy meant for harm, God intended to accomplish what is now being done—*"the saving of many lives."* The same is true for you. What has the enemy thrown at you? Where do you carry *forged-in-the-fire* authority to decree life? You are walking into new authority, my friend, and your decrees are releasing the God of Lazarus.

THE KING'S DECREE FOR YOU

"I am releasing resurrection life into every area that has felt dead or dry. I am pouring out awakening into your heart, My child. Resurrection life is flowing in abundance."
—THE KING

MY PRAYER FOR YOU

The Lord is moving in your life, friend. I bless all that He is doing. I ask for the resurrection power of Jesus to break forth in impossible circumstances, challenges, and obstacles that have tried to hinder your destiny, and I decree nothing is impossible with God in your life. I bless you to truly flourish and live fully alive. Every place the enemy has tried to contain you or keep you in grave clothes, I say, you are rising stronger. May bubbling joy that comes from God be a sign to you, that King Jesus is roaring resurrection life over your promises.

I pray the fire of God brands you, and I decree you are a burning one touched by the contagious fire of God for such a time as now. You are a Lazarus who has been raised from the dead; and I pray anointing on you to now go and do the same for others; bring many Lazarus circumstances out of the grave. I'm blessing your time with the Lord as precious, joy filled, and powerful. I bless you with Lazarus-style comebacks and turnarounds, in Jesus' name. Amen.

DECREE

- God is restoring my story and turning what the enemy meant for harm into good.

- There is no lack of resurrection power and creative solutions for my life.

- God is working all things together for my good.

- The same resurrection power that raised Jesus from the dead, lives in me.

- My voice is powerful, and I release resurrection life to dry and dead places, situations and people.

- I speak to Lazarus circumstances and they come out of the grave.

- I release resurrection life and hope everywhere I go.

Chapter 5

THE
TICKED-OFF ANGEL

And I am certain that God, who began the good work
within you, will continue his work until it is finally
finished on the day when Christ Jesus returns.
—Philippians 1:6 NLT

I think it's fair to say that I'm naturally a "fighter." What I mean is, my natural response to hard challenges is to battle in prayer and push through and find the silver lining. I have moments like everyone, but I'm not one to lie down and just accept impossible as the truth. I naturally look at impossible, and something rises within that says, "You just think you're impossible, but you, mountain of impossible, just need to meet the God who levels mountains!"

When Life Isn't What You Hoped

Many of my stories involve hospital rooms and urgent circumstances because that's been a big chunk of my life. It's precisely in our extreme moments of needing God that we find Him as our Redeemer. Like I often say, right before breakthrough, you know what things look like? The opposite of breakthrough!

After months on end of continual revival at "The Pineapple" and literally thousands of healings, the last place I expected to find myself was back in hospital with sudden and worsening symptoms. But there I was, in the emergency room and doctors were unable to offer anything encouraging. I am very grateful for the many doctors and nurses throughout my journey who have helped me. God has used them to partner with life and release medical healing and solutions many times. Some of my doctors became good friends as our hearts connected in some really hard seasons. I am so thankful for those in the medical profession who work tirelessly to help others.

If you are a medical professional, I bless you and speak anointed wisdom and skill on you, and that supernatural healing would partner with your anointed skills. I honor you and am grateful for you.

However, in *this* moment, doctors were gravely worried for me, medicine was not working, and they didn't have a medical solution, at least one that gave hope. My "insides" had just stopped working. I am aware of the questions that my situation caused for some. Having just been in the midst of so much glory, healings, and miracles, I understand it certainly was ironic to now need a miracle myself. All I can say is, it shows we are all in a battle. We found ourselves fighting well-worn tracks to speak life and urgent breakthrough over my health again. The name of Jesus is higher, and this was our decree.

Doctors informed Ben and me that things were extremely serious; and once again, we were faced with grim options to keep me alive, in their wise medical opinion. The prospect of having my entire bowel and portions of my stomach removed and feeding me through a tube was once again discussed. Success was considered slim due to complications and active disease.

On top of this, I was allergic to many of the medicines and drugs, adding to the pain and the problematic danger and nature of any treatment or surgery. At this point I couldn't eat at all, and even swallowing water had become a challenge. I was good in my soul, but I knew I needed a miracle, and quickly. The blessing of hosting revival and all that Jesus had done was that I'd never felt more alive, despite the circumstances.

Before I go on, I want to add a few thoughts on revival; what it is and what it isn't.

My Definition of Revival

Revival is a sudden outpouring of "reviving life" that returns the church to "normal," biblical Christianity where our hearts are fully on fire for Jesus and our faith is charged and revived to know that *"with God all things are possible"* (Matthew 19:26 NKJV). This is my user-friendly definition of revival.

A great example of revival in the Bible is when God poured out His Holy Spirit in the upper room and it resulted in *the* Church being established in fire, supernatural boldness, and passion, and souls were immediately won (Acts 2). Acts 2:46-47 tells us that the disciples continued to meet *every day* after this. There was something going on that was exciting enough to compel them to continue gathering, even with the Holy Spirit in them. When something "breaks out" in our midst on a corporate level, we call this revival, an outpouring, awakening, renewal. The word itself isn't really the important thing, it's that God is moving in a way that He wasn't a moment before, and lives are being impacted by God in a way that is life changing.

Sometimes the revival is citywide, or just for a church, or impacts an entire nation. When Jonah eventually did what God asked and released the message to Nineveh that God gave him, the entire city returned to God, an Old Testament type of awakening to God's truth, and revival of a city. The same happened in Jerusalem, as recorded in Acts. As the disciples shared the gospel with new power, it turned the entire city upside down and then impacted the nations, as they eventually *"went to the ends of the earth"* with the Good News (Acts 13:47 King James Version). We are *all* fruit of the ongoing impact of this revival!

PERSONAL REVIVAL

We are all called to live in personal revival. When corporate revivals happen, God is restoring to a people, region, or nation something we are lacking and in need of. He's reviving us to "first love" after Him, and then reviving our heart for others to have the same "first love" encounter with Him, restoring passion for souls. There may or may not be many salvations initially as God could be first causing His people to be on fire and sold out in their love for God, then salvations will follow automatically. It's a whole lot easier to evangelize when hearts are set on fire, let me tell you. We need revival because "we" need reviving, but also because the world needs to encounter a revived, on-fire church.

My personal definition of revival is that, "revival is the natural destination of hunger after Jesus that isn't squashed, stifled, contained, controlled, stomped on, resisted, opposed, or shut down"!

Boom! We ask for that God! Make us a transportable encounter of contagious hunger after Jesus.

We are all called to look like this:

> *Be enthusiastic to serve the Lord, keeping your passion toward him boiling hot! Radiate with the glow of the Holy Spirit and let him fill you with excitement as you serve him. Let this hope burst forth within you, releasing a continual joy. Don't give up in a time of trouble, but commune with God at all times* (Romans 12:11-12 TPT).

That Scripture passage from Romans 12 makes it pretty plain. We are all called to keep our passion boiling hot, not lukewarm, radiate His Spirit, be filled with excitement as we serve Him, hope bursting forth, exude continual joy, persevere in hard times, and be in constant heart connection to God regardless of what is going on. If we need some more of that anywhere in our life, then we need reviving! Revival, in all its expressions is reviving us to normal, biblical, on-fire, passionate Christianity! A continually revived church is a biblical church. To be personally "on-fire" is our intended normal temperature. Revival helps keep us "hot."

My point in saying all this—sometimes things happen that don't make sense and threaten to steal our hope. It doesn't mean God is not good or that revival isn't needed. Revival is *not* an instant fix-all of every issue, but it does speed up what God is doing and achieve a God-given purpose. Acceleration happens in revival as

God does something glorious in His presence that can only happen supernaturally. Revival isn't perfect, because people are involved. :) Have you ever met a perfect person? But it is glorious, worth everything, and a profound expression of the goodness and power of God to love on people and pour out His Spirit.

I can only say this, the Pineapple Revival was the most glorious, holy, power-filled, fiery, heart-stirring, Jesus-honoring, life-changing, and awe-inspiring time I've ever walked through. God said to Ben and me one day, "To you who's had more, there's still more!" He surely poured out more, *and I'm still hungry!*

Our world needs Jesus. I am also aware that we are on the cusp of the greatest awakening we have ever seen. Every revival that you've ever been in or heard of will pale in comparison to what God is about to pour out. The "pent-up flood" of His Spirit and glory is about to astound us all.

> *...For he will come like a pent-up flood that the breath of the Lord drives along* (Isaiah 59:19).

I often say that it's *not* selfish, foolish, or immature to go after the "more" of God. Indeed, it's in fact a biblical response to a lost world to pursue being *"boiling hot."* The world needs hearts on fire for Jesus and nothing less will do, as literal eternities are at stake.

The harvest is so urgent that we need everything and everyone we've got. It's time to stop having competing values and agendas and realize it's *not* "either or" in this season, rather it's "both and more"! It's not holiness or the glory. It's not the Word or the supernatural. It's not evangelism or revival. It's not fear of the Lord or joy. It's not rest or contending. It's not prayer or taking action. It's not tears or laughter. It's not justice or mercy. It's not grace or righteousness. It's all of that—and more! Maturity says, it's both and more.

BOOKS AND HEAVENLY SCROLLS

What I do know is, it wasn't God's heart for me to be unwell, and it wasn't revival's fault. There's only one thief who comes to *"steal and kill and destroy"* (John 10:10 NLT) and it's definitely *not* God.

I knew I had promises still to walk out, and I began systematically remembering and speaking out those promises in prayer. I decreed, "God, You know my promises; I ask You to remember them God and read them out in Heaven!"

God remembers, and like any good Father, He has them recorded in Heaven. Psalm 139:16 (NLT) says, *"You saw me before I was born. Every day of my life was recorded in your book. Every moment was laid out before a single day had passed."* I love how The Passion Translation puts it: *"You saw who you created me to be before I became me! Before I'd ever seen the light of day, the number of days you planned for me were already recorded in your book."*

God indeed has books in Heaven, or scrolls if you like, whatever we want to call them. Scripture says God keeps a record of our days and our promises. God remembers your promises and writes them in a book. Our heavenly Father has dreams for us, destiny promises, plans made from the throne room that are only for us and fashioned with us in mind before we were even born. Wow, think about that! Then God records them in Heaven and they are written there now.

What an incredibly attentive God we have who records every day and moment, and has them systematically laid out. God saw who He created you to be before you became you! Those words are mind-blowing. But the point is, God has recorded our promises, remembers them, and knows what we are purposed and made for, and what brings us to life. This truth is incredibly comforting and loving. What a doting Father we have as our God.

God's Promises

I've been marked over the years by the story of Moses in the tent of meeting and his discussions with God as his Friend. I was moved by Moses' ability to "reason" with God and influence circumstances, even influence God's decisions for the nation. These conversations between a man and the King actually affected outcomes. I was equally marked by knowing that God has our promises recorded in Heaven and *"God is not a man, so he does not lie"* (Numbers 23:19 NLT). My prayers reflected this over and over as I decreed, "Open your scrolls, God. Open up the scrolls of Heaven and read out the promises recorded for my life. Read them out in Heaven, God, and remember what You have promised." I knew what God decreed must be fulfilled here on earth, and so I prayed, shouted, pronounced, and whispered.

Don't get me wrong, there were many hard moments, times of tears, and moments I found it hard to even open my mouth except to cry. Ben was my greatest strength in these moments. I know there are many battles I quite simply would not have won if it were not for my husband and his constant love and refusal to settle for anything less than breakthrough. I'm blessed and thankful for him in my life. To have a husband who battles with you in the moments when your greatest fears seem to be knocking at the door, that's a treasured blessing.

It's not always been easy, far from it, but we have faced challenges together.

Ben and I would walk down—well, he pushed my wheelchair and intravenous drip, as I was too weak to walk—down to the hospital chapel. That was a hard moment when I realized I couldn't walk anymore. I knew I needed God to show up. We'd "sneak away" to the chapel, which was surprisingly always empty, and we'd pray and worship. I needed this time "away" to recalibrate my heart and lean into God's promises. We also prayed for everyone else in the hospital who needed a miracle.

My heart cry was simple: "God, You are still the God of Lazarus, and Your arm is not too short to reach me. So I decree life to the dead places in my body. I've seen You do it before. I've seen You do for hundreds of others. So I speak resurrection power over my life."

I'd decreed this decree maybe thousands of times as we ministered, now I was decreeing it over myself. "Just like Moses talked to You, God," I'd say, "I'm asking You to remember my promises You have recorded and speak them out in Heaven! You remember, God," I would shout out, "YOU SPEAK OUT MY PROMISES. CALL THEM OUT BY NAME. YOU'VE DONE IT BEFORE—DO IT AGAIN!"

His presence was close. I felt Him so near. But I was tired, so tired of the pain and the battle.

As complication after complication in my body was getting worse not better, and my insides felt as though they were on fire, I was really struggling in myself. I was in constant, extreme pain; and honestly, I felt at the end of my ability to fight, mostly because the pain was constant. I was struggling.

I remember one night as Ben was saying goodnight, I just cried as I couldn't find words anymore. I asked Ben to ask people to pray as I instinctively knew that I needed others to contend with us that night, to fight alongside us. Keely prayed too as did count-less others. To fight alongside someone in prayer is the greatest of gifts. I knew God's closeness and realness, but I was exhausted and weak. My only response was tears.

Our Tears Are Liquid Intercession

Lord, you know all my desires and deepest longings. My tears are liquid words and you can read them all (Psalm 38:9 TPT).

How beautiful is that verse? And how tender. I tell you, there is something wonderful about knowing God as the One who reads our tears like liquid intercession. When our words have run out, He reads our tears and translates our heart's deepest longings. Our tears are *liquid words*.

On this night, as I lay in extreme pain and exhaustion, it was one of those moments…my tears became my decree. Let the ten-derness of God speak to the deepest part of *your* heart, my friend. We serve the God who *"is close to the brokenhearted"* (Psalm 34:18). The Passion Translation states it this way, *"The Lord is close to all whose hearts are crushed by pain."* The "realness" of God breaks my heart sometimes. He is so much more loving and kind, and near than we realize.

My point is, if the only decree you can make sometimes is a tear, then cry in His presence and let Him translate your liquid words. Your liquid decrees are powerful too. God "reads" your tears. I pray the closeness of Heaven and nearness of God holding you in the realness of your hardest, most challenging moments, when you don't have words left. In these moments, I pray you will know even then, that God is with you and is releasing supernatural answers.

Just know that He knows. Breathe in hope, my friend. God knows, He's moving, and He cares. God is not limited by impossible circumstances. When things are at the worst, you are positioned for a miracle solution.

SUDDENLY

Alone in my hospital room at around midnight, I knew Ben had sent out an urgent request for prayer. One of those requests was on Facebook, and I was amazed that suddenly there were thousands of people praying. How grateful I was. I started to feel a shift in the atmosphere. My body was in extreme pain still and the worst was the "burning sensation." I'd had a reaction to some medications and my insides felt like acid was burning me—but the atmosphere in my hospital room felt "charged."

Suddenly I received a text with a word from a dear friend and "father" of ours, Paul Manwaring who is on the leadership team at Bethel Church in Redding, California.

> *Fear not, for I have redeemed you; I have called you by your name; You are Mine. When you pass through the waters, I will be with you; And through the rivers, they shall not overflow you. When you walk through the fire, you shall not be burned, nor shall the flame scorch you* (Isaiah 43:1-2 NKJV).

Paul didn't know the exact details—that I was having a reaction and felt burning pain inside. He also didn't know I was asking God to remember my promises by name. Yet these verses spoke directly to me. Immediately faith "hit" me, and within minutes, the fire sensation was gone completely!

I knew God was up to something. As I lay in the hospital bed feeling the atmosphere charged, and for the first time, pain reduced. I knew I was in the beginning of a "suddenly."

Suddenly, with my eyes open I saw an angel in the corner of my hospital room. The more I looked, the clearer I saw. The atmosphere was thick with glory. I was aware this angel had been sent from the throne room and the presence of God.

I was actually overcome with emotion. All I could do was cry, except now they were tears of relief, as I said over and over, "You've come, God, I knew You'd come. I knew You'd read out my name. I knew You would come God...I knew You would come." My spirit leapt. There was a crispness in the atmosphere, an electricity that I recognized immediately from other encounters I'd had from the throne room of Heaven. My insides were "buzzing" with that familiar feeling of the charged, supernatural power of God.

A TICKED-OFF ANGEL

I was intrigued by this angel. As only happens in the middle of an encounter, I was transfixed as something from the throne room was unfolding. I looked and could see the angel was holding a clipboard and pen and was staring at me, almost looking angry. This would have bothered me except for the fact that the presence of God was so thick and so heavy, it only caused me to wonder what was going on as the look on the angel's face was so stern and fierce.

Some friends of ours, Dan Hagen and Ben Fitzgerald, suddenly and randomly felt led to phone me from the other side of the world and rebuke all torment and affliction in the name of Jesus. It was a powerful prayer. I felt something shift again and more pain eased. I looked at the angel who now seemed more relaxed, and it hit me that the angel had not been looking angry at me, but was angry at the torment the devil had been inflicting on me. This "ticked-off angel" as I have come to call it, was ticked off at the devil!

I watched the angel grab the pen and tick off something on the clipboard it was holding, it was a checklist as others would say. This was curious to me but seemed very important and official. This angel was systematically ticking things off a list.

I could feel the stirring of expectancy and I knew people were praying all around the world right then, including my family who never gave up. I knew this because many, many people suddenly started messaging, or later messaged, saying how in that very moment they suddenly felt compelled to pray. How grateful I am for the body, the Church. Words don't express that adequately enough.

I just "knew" I was getting better. I had a feeling in my body that I could get well now. I felt peaceful and able to rest, which was a miracle. I looked again at the angel and watched something else on the list get ticked off.

As only possible in an encounter or vision, I could suddenly see the clipboard and I saw a very long list of promises. I realized this was a list of my promises from Heaven! God had opened up the scrolls in Heaven and sent an angel from the throne room with a list of my promises that are recorded in Heaven. This angel was standing in my hospital room ticking off my promises one after the other after the other! I wept uncontrollably. I couldn't believe it when I realized, "God, You heard me and remembered my promises."

I could see the long, *long* list, but I couldn't read the promises. Yet I knew they were *all* my promises and God had not forgotten a single one. I somehow knew they were in order and God was ticking off promise after promise in a divine order and timing that was perfect and aligned. I could trust Him with my promises. I could trust Him to complete them. I could trust Him with the timing. Nothing was forgotten or out of order, and every word spoken over my life was there on this clipboard, that I knew had come from the very records in Heaven.

Malachi 3:16 says, *"Then those who feared the Lord talked with each other, and the Lord listened and heard. A scroll of remembrance was written in his presence concerning those who feared the Lord and honored his name."* I often thought of this verse and imagined scrolls in Heaven, books of remembrance that contained our names and stories of us honoring the Lord. I often even now stop when I'm overwhelmed with thanks and pray, "Would You record in Heaven that I'm thankful right now, God. Thank You for doing that."

In front of my eyes, in the corner of the room, I continued to watch the angel systematically mark off from the records of Heaven every word ever spoken over my life It was overwhelming, it was holy, it was so incredible to see before my eyes the faithfulness of the King. I was aware of the intimacy of the moment. We are known by name, and He knows us completely. Not one promise is forgotten.

It was then when I suddenly *saw* a huge eagle arrive. I was unaware at this point if this was a vision, or real. It was surreal. My eyes were open. I was awake. I could see my hospital room and the angel in the corner, and yet I also was aware of the superimposing of another realm. The eagle's talons were sharp and fierce, and my eye was drawn to them. I knew that somehow this eagle was here to destroy the works of the enemy.

I looked and watched the angel tick off another promise.

I heard a voice speak and simply say, "This is a blessing of Obed-Edom" (2 Samuel 6:12). "Those who honor My presence shall be blessed." This statement made me cry. Oh how I loved

God's presence. Revival had done nothing to satisfy our hunger for His presence; if anything, it had made us hungrier. And at the same time, I was extremely aware that without God's grace, none of us are worthy. I had a touch of the fear of the Lord before, and I could suddenly feel that same holiness again. Our King is a holy King, and holiness matters. His presence is glorious and I felt it fall like a heavy blanket. I was marked afresh. I sensed the fear of the Lord infuse the room that isn't fear at all, it was hunger for more. Even in that moment I desired more of His presence.

Again as I watched the angel, more was being ticked off the list.

I was aware of feeling expectant in my body. I still felt unwell, but I had a surge of hope from Heaven. For what seemed like a long time, this encounter lingered and God's presence was heavy. I was aware things were happening that I could not see or understand, but were imperative and significant.

As I *watched* at different moments, the angel was still standing guard in the corner of my hospital room and ticking off more promises. I was aware there were many more promises yet, some for now, some for seasons to come, but all were recorded, all would be completed in due time. Nothing was missing. Nothing forgotten.

I suddenly was very sleepy. I knew there was more to complete in my body and more promises to tick off yet. I looked up at the angel and there was such peace and yet fierce determination that what needed to happen was getting done. I heard an inner voice, "What needs to happen is better that you are asleep now." I would have worried about hearing that except the peace I felt right then was so rich and deep. This whole encounter was surreal, and yet more real than real. It was like I'd stepped into a dream and yet I was fully awake. As I drifted off to sleep, I took a last look in the corner of my room, and the angel was still standing guard, pen in hand and ticking more things off the list on the clipboard.

And then suddenly, it was early morning and a nurse was waking me up and taking my "obs," medical observations to check how I was. She was very happy, saying everything was normal and seemed quite surprised. I immediately looked over toward the corner of the room. I couldn't see the angel anymore, but I knew the tick list of my promises was still being watched over, guarded, enacted, and being completed.

I felt good. There was enough immediate change in my body that I knew something had changed. I got up and was incredibly given the go-ahead to try and eat, and wow, I ate easily. I was starving.

The night before was etched in my heart. God remembers and is completing every promise on my life I was saying over and over.

Well, later that same day, miraculously I was discharged from the hospital. Only 24 hours earlier I thought my life was slipping away. It was quite the sudden turnaround. Doctors were amazed. I was still improving moment by moment, and it was obvious to everyone something had dramatically changed. I was given the all-clear to go home.

Now do you want to hear the kicker? This just made me laugh at the enemy and praise God all the more! Guess what the doctor's name was who discharged me from hospital that day. You'll never guess—Dr. Lazarus! Yes, really! I mean, come on! God is just too incredible. How profoundly prophetic.

God, You are still the God who brings Lazarus circumstances out of the grave and brings life to dead places in our lives. For nothing is impossible with You, God, including the impossible!

I left the hospital very weak and barely able to support my own weight walking, but so excited knowing a miraculous turnaround had just taken place and that the King had decreed completion of every promise He had begun.

You know where I went that night? Church! Back to the Pineapple Revival! I couldn't wait to be in His presence and worship and thank Him for what He had done, and all He was still doing. I remember sitting on a beanbag at the front of church and crying tears of thanks. What a great God we serve!

The miracle didn't stop there.

Wave of Awakening

A few days later, as a family we flew to Hawaii on a pre-planned holiday that we thought we were going to have to forfeit because of my health. How kind is God. Not only did I get on that plane, I was feeling stronger every day.

Here's something crazy I just have to tell you. As we arrived in Hawaii and were taken to our hotel room, we were given an upgrade. We'd never been to Hawaii before. I looked out the window and we had a stunning view all the way up Waikiki Beach. It took my breath away, but not just because it was beautiful. I suddenly had a *kairos* moment of "right place, right time," as I was aware that I'd seen this scene before.

Seven years previously I had had a vivid dream of being at a beach in Hawaii and seeing a huge wave of revival and harvest sweep the globe. I couldn't believe it as I looked and knew that this was the same beach I had been standing on. I'd been here before in my dream. It was surreal. It was exactly as I remembered it. How incredible that I had that dream and then went to the exact place right after extended revival, and God miraculously released breakthrough to get me there! That dream was about a worldwide harvest and unprecedented revival. We are in the beginnings of that era now.

This says to me that not only does God complete what He promises, but that the timing of God is perfect. He is always on time. He knows what He's doing. And we are in a season of harvest and awakening. Be expectant. Let your heart stir with hope and your mouth be filled with praise. Everything God has begun in you, He will faithfully continue, complete, and add the "finishing touches."

> *I pray with great faith for you, because I'm fully convinced that the One who began this glorious work in you will faithfully continue the process of maturing you and will put his finishing touches to it until the unveiling of our Lord Jesus Christ!* (Philippians 1:6 TPT)

THE KING'S DECREE FOR YOU

"My child, I have begun something good in you and I am always faithful to complete every work. I will finish what I have started. Rest in My faithfulness."
—THE KING

MY PRAYER FOR YOU

Every promise recorded over your life, I call into fullness of completion in the name of Jesus. I ask for increase of encounters that breathe hope and release peace to your heart and mind. I say you are marked for glory, abundant life, fulfillment, and peace, healing, and miracles. You are a sign and a wonder of the ability of God to resurrect stories and breathe new life where the enemy thought he won. Be expectant, faithful one; I bless you with supernatural solutions and miraculous turnarounds. God has you covered with His love. He is an impenetrable shield of protection, and He remembers your promises. I bless those promises to be completed in Jesus' name. Amen.

DECREE

- I decree all things are possible, even what seems impossible.
- I call in every promise that is recorded in Heaven for my life, my family, and my nation.
- Everything God has begun He is faithful to complete.
- My voice activates what the King has spoken.

Chapter 6

YOUR VOICE IS POWERFUL

*Receive this truth: Whatever you forbid on earth will be
considered to be forbidden in heaven, and whatever you
release on earth will be considered to be released in heaven.*
—MATTHEW 18:18 TPT

Your voice. Your decrees. Your words. Your faith. Your prayers are
affecting change!

"Charge your weapons, bride of Christ, and receive this truth."
I have heard this phrase over and over in my spirit lately, as the
King announces this truth upgrade. Whatever *you* forbid and *you*
release will be considered forbidden or released! *You* are empowered and powerful. *You* are called to partner with God's word and
impact what is released from Heaven on the earth. Your voice is
essential and part of the process. The enemy has tried to steal your

voice for far too long; and in this season, the shackles are coming off! Get ready, mighty one! Intimidation is breaking across the body of Christ as fresh authority comes on the interceding prophetic voice of the Church.

> *"**You** will also decree a thing, and it will be established for **you**…"* (Job 22:28 NASB).

Your voice is being raised up in new power to declare and establish. God is restoring your story and writing new redemptive solutions into your destiny as you move in faith, and decree His promises.

All that the enemy has stolen, messed with, or broken, God is redeeming. New stories of "things working together for good" are being written even now, in the places that felt forgotten or unredeemable. Your best days are before you, and brokenness is not your future. There are exploits of incredible courage and breakthrough in the seasons to come that will impact our sphere of influence mightily, that your voice is establishing now as you decree and declare a thing, and as you forbid and release! Yes, the prayers of others are powerful, but so are yours!

There is nothing more powerful in your world, than your voice. You, partnering with God's word and speaking truth is not only powerful, but crucial. Your voice is a secret weapon, often the secret ingredient of breakthrough that the enemy wants silenced.

Your voice is powerful and that's why the enemy has attempted to silence you. God is weaponizing your voice and unleashing you as a faith detonator and chain breaker. Your voice is part of the solution that is unfolding as you establish the Kingdom through your decrees and prayers.

God is uncapping your potential and unleashing the faith within you to partner with Heaven and establish God's glory on the earth—specifically in your sphere of influence. Sometimes just starting something is the biggest part of the battle; so use these pages to speak out decrees and realign your faith with the God who levels mountains.

Matthew 18:18 (TPT) says, *"Receive this truth: Whatever you forbid on earth will be considered to be forbidden in heaven, and whatever you release on earth will be considered to be released in heaven."*

Let's really read that *you* is mentioned twice in that verse. Your voice is invited to partner with God in establishing His truth in and around you. This is not just an invitation, however, it's a directive extended to us from the King Himself to establish this truth deep in our core. Our declarations affect the world around us, and God considered our decrees powerful enough that Heaven leans in and partners with us! It follows that as we marinate in the truth of this Scripture, it shifts from an invitation to a clarion call of compelling hope that praying this way changes things. We will no longer be satisfied with generic prayers; rather, we will desire to know the heart of God and speak forth what God is saying.

RELEASE WHAT YOU CARRY

I often think of the story of David and Goliath, as this giant was speaking out intimidating threats and heaping fear over an entire nation. Then David comes along, a young boy really, but bold in his experience of God being with him through past life-threatening moments. He simply believed God was greater than the enemy, no matter how big the giant looked.

You probably know the story well; David, who was just taking lunch to his brothers, ended up changing a nation! Determined to see freedom, David took five stones and flung one right at Goliath, which hit the mark and Goliath fell down dead, releasing a nation from the tyranny of fear. Those stones were nothing amazing, just rocks. They were just what David had in his hand. He had built a confidence in using what was at his disposal. It wasn't until they were released and thrown in the direction of the giant, though, that they became weaponized. The stones needed to be thrown and released deliberately to take out the enemy.

Our voice is similar in that we build bold faith as we use it. Eventually, we build up a history with the Lord as each giant comes down! Declarations not spoken, are like stones not thrown at Goliath. As we open our mouths and speak, pointing our "stones" in the direction of the enemy, we weaponize our words— and remember, our fight *"is not against flesh and blood* [people], *but against the rulers, against the authorities, against the powers of this dark world and against the spiritual forces of evil in the heavenly realms"* (Ephesians 6:12). Again, our fight is not directed at people, we are decreeing truth to spiritual forces.

Picking up our weapons and purposefully throwing them looks like opening our mouths, and directing our intercession at the Goliaths that still arrogantly stand and threaten the body, the Church. But the power is in the speaking out, proclaiming out, decreeing out, and actively releasing truth as a faith-directed weapon that smashes the lies of the enemy. Release the weapon God has given you, your voice!

The stones David threw at the giant had to be thrown! Just looking at the stones or holding the stones did nothing to slay the giant. David needed to actively throw the stones with the intent of taking out Goliath, and it's the same with our decrees and intercession. The only inactive prayers are the ones we don't actually pray.

Speak it out! Release it! There is power in speaking out, releasing truth, and activating our faith to release what God is saying with *our own voice*. What are the "goliaths" in your world or nation that you are actively taking aim at with your intercession?

There is a call going out that is urging the inner warrior in us all to pick up our prophetic stones and throw them at the arrogance of the enemy that would dare to threaten a child of the King with intimidation. There are fields of latent destiny all around awaiting the ones whose voices will tell those dry bones to get up (Ezekiel 37), or speak to the fields of unfinished stories and say, "God isn't finished with you yet." The only decrees that aren't effective, are the ones that aren't released.

A MIRACLE THAT SPEAKS

A lady came for prayer at the Pineapple Revival whom I have never forgotten. She walked up holding a handwritten sign that simply read, "I can't talk. I have tumors in my throat. I need a miracle. Please pray." Compassion rose up, and I prayed a simple prayer, "God, would You come heal her and give her back her voice." The woman dropped to the ground as though dead, and remained that way until the end of the meeting. We left her alone as it was obvious God was doing something. As we were packing up at the end, ready to go home, this lady came running up to me and said, "Thank you so much for praying!" I was about to answer, when it struck me she was talking and I said with a laugh, "You can't talk?!" to which she replied, "I can now!"

Wow, we both were astounded and thanked God. She came back to the revival a few times over the next months to update us that the tumors had completely disappeared and she was totally healed. She would always tell us, "I'm still speaking!" How kind is God? He literally healed her and restored her voice! I've always thought this miracle speaks loudly to the body right now. God is giving us—His Bride—our voices back. And if He has to heal some things, and remove some obstructions or obstacles to do that, He will and He is. God is amplifying the voice of the praying Church right now, and revival fire is restoring the cutting edge of the bride's decrees.

THE NATION NOTICED

When Moses entered the tent of meeting, as he did regularly to talk to the Lord, Scripture records that the glory of the Lord was seen as a literal glory cloud that came down on the tent for the duration of their conversation. The King met with His son, the reluctant leader; and while they spoke, a literal glory cloud was seen by the whole nation. In fact, the people would know when Moses was talking to God by whether or not they could see glory over their meeting place. Wow! Something about Moses attracted the glory of God in such a way that it manifested in a "seen" way.

Moses' interactions, his conversations with the King attracted the presence of God in such a way that an entire nation knew their leader was actively seeking God. In other words, people always knew when Moses was talking with God because it was obvious, observable, and seen! Their friendship and conversations impacted the entire nation. I often think of this, and ask myself: *Are my conversations with God impacting those around me? Can people "see" the glory of God emanate from me because I've been talking to God? Does my friendship with the Holy Spirit benefit others? Does it benefit my family and city as I hear God's heart? Is God's presence observable in how I do life? Can people "see" the fruit of my friendship with God in real ways?*

"Tent of meeting" conversations are not confined to Moses' and Joshua's day. We live in a better covenant, and so what Moses had is available to us as the starting place, not the ceiling. We carry His presence within us and so we are mobile "tents of meeting" with continual access to the Holy Spirit. Moses came from his cloud-of-glory conversations with God fresh with strategies and revelation for the nation. We too are invited to come away from meeting with the Lord and know His heart to declare, to have strategies that bring solutions. This should be our expectation.

Of course like any friendship, not every conversation contains strategies, as sometimes we are simply enjoying each other's company; but the fact remains that tent-of-meeting conversations gave Moses God's heart *to decree something and establish it*, and this led a nation into destiny. This same interaction is available to us, including nation-shifting declarations and strategies from God. But let's not forget, God equally has strategies, ideas, promises, solutions, and revelation to declare over our children, our parents, our jobs, our calling, our finances, our bodies, our creative thinking...it goes on and on to include every aspect of our lives.

We are designed to desire friendship with the King, and come from our tent-of-meeting encounters with His heart to speak into our circumstances. Our friendship with God has the power to impact nations and reflect a tangible residue of His glory—so much so that at the very least those around us are impacted by the residue of God's glory from our time with Him. It's a challenging thought to think that our friendship with God should benefit our sphere of influence. God's heart revealed in our time spent with Him will naturally impact our prayer life, and result in decreeing *"a thing, and it will be established for you"* (Job 22:28 NASB).

It's from this place of intimate connection that all else flows, including the power to speak to that which needs to get in line with the Word of God.

What I've discovered is, God is more than eager to invite you into a "tent of meeting" with His heart so that you can be a voice of influence and authority decreeing on behalf of the King. He's eager to hear your thoughts and speak to all manner of situations, heart processing, and circumstances requiring divine wisdom and supernatural power. He loves to chat with you, and enjoys your company. He also invites us to know divine secrets, His thinking on a matter, and the inner thoughts of His heart (John 15:15 TPT).

This kind of friendship with the King changes everything. It changes our prayer life. It changes how we decree. For no longer are we decreeing from a place of just hope, we are declaring from a faith of knowing the heart of our King and our words carry the authority of the King backing us up. Our conversations with the Lord have now become prophetic declarations of *now* faith from the courts of Heaven. The words spoken with our own voice, our faith, are now truly edicts from the King of kings; and as any edict, it *must* be decreed.

What a great honor to steward the King's heart well; and once hearing His thoughts, be ones who will release what He is saying. I'm cautioned here to say that when our decrees come from time in His presence, it's equally important that our prayers carry not just the words, but the heart of God. It's an honor beyond honors to share in the secrets and mysteries of Heaven. May we honor His heart well and endeavor to convey this with the same heart He spoke it in.

I am often reminded in sharing God's heart to be careful to not add any "little extras" to what I am sensing Him saying and do my best to keep the message pure and true to His heart intentions. It's equally important to remember that nothing God says will ever contradict, violate, or dishonor His written Word, the Bible. His Word is not only a wise foundation, but an essential ingredient to this journey. The Bible is the written, inspired Word of God and the foundation of our faith. It's more than words on a page—the Bible is living, active, and "God breathed" (see Hebrews 4:12 and 2 Timothy 3:16).

The Bible consists of the only words you can read that are actually *"alive and active"*:

> *For the word of God is alive and active. Sharper than any double-edged sword, it penetrates even to dividing soul and spirit, joints and marrow; it judges the thoughts and attitudes of the heart* (Hebrews 4:12).

Someone in love with the King, will also grow in love for His written Word. I will say, however, God can, and will, talk to "the world" whether they know little, lots, or none of His written Word. God doesn't check how much of the Bible people know before He starts a conversation with a hurting world.

A Catalytic Vision

In 2018 I had a profound vision for the new era the Church was entering that marked me. I saw a bride dressed and ready, wielding strong and effective weapons. The weapon she used was her voice.

As she spoke, I saw the dark clouds part and light pierce through the darkness. The bride was shouting, announcing, and decreeing, "On earth as it is in my Father's house" (Matthew 6:10). Her voice was not timid, reserved, or unsure—it was bold, wild, and determined. As I watched the bride use her voice as a weapon, a resolve came upon her, and with a loud shout she yelled, "ENOUGH!"

The vision then changed and I saw multitudes awaken. They came from the caves, the wilderness, from the threshing field and the mountaintops, each bore wounds and scars, but they came forth at the sound of the bride's shout. As the multitudes gathered, they turned into an army, standing to attention, immediately ready for war. I looked and saw the warrior bride, her face toward Heaven; and again I saw her raise her weapon, releasing her shout.

This time she commanded, "CHARGE!" At the intensity of her command, the army dropped to their knees and like thunder, *one voice* was raised to Heaven. Their voice, as a weapon, was sharper than any sword I'd ever seen. The bride then shouted one last impassioned command, "CHARGE, YOU WARRIORS, CHARGE YOUR WEAPONS, VICTORY IS IN SIGHT!"

> *Look at all the people coming—now is harvest time* (John 4:35 TPT).

The message of this vision is simple. It's time to charge your weapons. It's time for the bride of Christ to proclaim, "Now is the time of harvest." Your voice is writing history, your courage is shifting nations, your prayers are effecting change, your decrees are releasing breakthrough. The army of God is arising and there's a new breed of fierce warrior awakened who knows how to wield their voices as a weapon. There's an intercession revolution taking place before our eyes as the mighty, decreeing bride finds her voice.

And so, *"Whatever you forbid on earth will be considered to be forbidden in heaven, and whatever you release on earth will be considered to be released in heaven."* Wow, is probably the only worthy response. What trust God is placing in you, His friend. What very great belief He has in you. As His Kingdom ambassador, He partners with you, your words and decrees on behalf of Himself to forbid and release Heaven's edicts. Essentially, *you* are speaking things into being, establishing His Word and Kingdom truths, and releasing supernatural shifts that bring God-change wherever you go.

People we do not know and will never meet will benefit from the prayers we release after tent-of-meeting conversations with God. This compels me to open my mouth and speak! We have one life, and yet we have the opportunity to affect countless lives and generations to come as we decree, "Enough," and speak out "as it is in my Father's house."

I pause for a moment and acknowledge the many faithful prayers from the generations before us that we are still living in the benefit and fruit from now. Just that thought alone is enough to compel us to want to rise and decree into the days, seasons, and generations to come. Our children and those yet to be born, will live in the benefit and fruit of the prayers we decree today. This is *powerful!* Our prayers shape history!

You might be in circumstances that you think are small and wonder how effectual your life has been. I'm telling you, your voice is powerful and your declarations can speak to generations not yet born and affect *"nations you know not"* (Isaiah 55:5). Your prayers can, and are, shifting governments and laws, and calling back original destiny over families, cities, and cultural foundations.

New medical discoveries, national economic turnarounds, divine strategies for global injustices, miracle breakthroughs, inventions that affect ground-breaking change, entire nations saved in a day, and the future destiny of your own family—all this can be influenced, released, and established by those who know their God. Multitudes of souls are effected by the decrees of those who understand that their voice is powerful. And all this comes from a conversation between a King and His friend.

None of this makes sense outside of the truth that we are loved by God and cultivating a personal and authentic relationship with the Holy Spirit. How can we know God's heart and decree God's heart without knowing God? It all starts there. And how can we stay true to the full counsel of the Lord if we do not have a love for His Word? And just knowing that it's possible to have an ongoing, current, interactive, real conversation with the King of kings who is our heavenly Father and our Friend, is compelling.

Beyond that, we need to know that our own voice carries power to shift circumstances, and God has empowered us to partner with Him in the greatest of destiny-shaping, mountain-shifting adventures. Establish that *you* will release what the King is saying. *Your* voice is powerful, anointed, and carries the authority of the King. Even in the quietness of your prayer room, bedroom, cafe table, or wherever, as you whisper His heart with seemingly no one hearing, your voice is releasing words of life that break chains and echo into eternity.

If you really believe your prayer life impacts nations and generations to come, what will you pray today? How would you pray? Would you decree with more boldness and prioritize prayer differently? If you really believe your voice is powerful, how will this affect your prayer and decrees for your family and nation?

LET THERE BE LIGHT

God showed me just how powerful our decrees are in a wild way.

When my husband and I were in Nadi, Fiji, in 2011 ministering, we were part of a revival that broke out. We watched all kinds of amazing miracles happen almost instantly, including blind eyes see, deaf ears open, many people giving their lives to God, signs and wonders like sudden strong winds that blew over all the chairs inside the church, 6-foot flames of fire seen on the stage, supernatural rain, angels singing, all kinds of healings and deliverance happening—glorious sums it up! Revival was truly breaking out.

One night I had not been feeling well and stayed home. I was alone in the bedroom and I could feel the battle in the atmosphere for continued breakthrough. I was in my room with all the lights off and it was dark, which is important to know. Suddenly, an intense "darkness" moved in. I was aware of a thick, ominous darkness and evil presence that came around our apartment and the atmosphere became like a thick fog that was trying to settle. Though it was dark in the room, I felt darkness arrive, and with it a tangible fear. It seemed every dog in the region suddenly started barking viciously as I sensed an eerie, foreboding fear.

I became immediately alert and stood to my feet to pray, knowing this was a show of force from the enemy to prevent a continued move of God. I jumped up out of bed and literally shouted, "LET THERE BE LIGHT" and began praying and marching around my bedroom. Sensing the urgency of the moment in the spirit, I shouted boldly again and decreed loudly, "LET THERE BE LIGHT!"

Immediately, the en suite bathroom light came on by itself! My bedroom was suddenly lit up and full of light, and at the same time the evil presence and thick darkness in the atmosphere instantly dissipated. The dark that had been darker than dark receded, and strangely, every dog immediately stopped barking, too. A thick, peaceful silence descended.

I stood in my now lit-up apartment thanking God for His goodness; and honestly, a little shocked at the practical demonstration God gave me of the power of our decrees!

Commanding, "Let there be light" shifted the darkness and released the light in more ways than one that evening! I later found out that the meeting went to a new level that night too with salvation and healings flowing after much "warfare"! I've never forgotten this moment! Always remember, *your voice is powerful!* This practical sign and wonder marked me from that day. Our decrees shift things. Decree light to the darkness in your world as your prayers change things.

THE KING'S DECREE FOR YOU

"My child, whatever you bind on earth, I consider to be bound in Heaven; and whatever you release on earth, I consider to be released in Heaven. I have given you authority to decree My voice to the world around you."
—THE KING

MY PRAYER FOR YOU

I'm praying for a new awareness of how anointed your voice is, courageous one. Contained in you are prayers that break chains in your family and release destiny in your generation. I am decreeing bold, wild, fiery, nation-shaking faith over you. Your praise is shifting the atmosphere and activating miracles in your circumstances, family, and community. I ask for more. I ask for breakthroughs that completely amaze you at how good God is.

You're anointed to thrive in your life and calling, and I pray fire on your words and heart. Wherever you go, the King goes, and your prayers are evicting darkness and releasing light. I speak unparalleled glory breaking into your life, and infusing your heart and home right now. In Jesus' name, amen.

DECREE

- My voice is powerful. I release light and evict darkness in Jesus' name.
- Whatever I bind on earth will be bound in Heaven. Whatever I release on earth will be released in Heaven. I am a releaser of Heaven's atmosphere and the glory of God.
- My voice, decrees, words, and prayers are effecting change right now.
- I decree that everything in my hand belongs to You, God.
- I will not hold back my voice; I will release it.
- Your authority as the King is backing me up! I will run. I will fight. I will take those giants down. I will live in victory.
- My voice slays the giants in my world.

Chapter 7

CONTENDING 101

*That's why I plead with you, because of our union with our
Lord Jesus Christ, to be partners with me in your prayers to
God. My dear brothers and sisters in the faith, with the love
we share in the Holy Spirit, fight alongside me in prayer.*
—ROMANS 15:30 TPT

Behind every answer to prayer, outbreak of miracles, and revival
is a praying people. And behind every "suddenly" is usually a long
road of consistent surrender, persevering, and the unseen cost
of contending.

There is often a contending, or a "fight alongside in prayer"
to enter the fullness of some breakthroughs. Even in the natural,
endurance and faithfulness is often an under-appreciated prerequisite of success. Truly, our faithful "every days" set us up for our
"one days"!

Jesus explained to the disciples in Mark 9:29 that there were some breakthroughs that required *prayer and fasting* to achieve. He encouraged His disciples who had not been able to deliver the young boy when they prayed for him, and then Jesus immediately brought freedom. Jesus is always our Coach, Cheerleader, and example of what is possible. This spurs us on that if there is a challenge that we've not seen breakthrough in yet, there is biblical encouragement to press in and contend to see. It also says there are breakthroughs to contend for that we haven't even thought of praying for yet.

Contending is often misunderstood, seen as unnecessary, or considered lack of faith. Sadly some attack or judge the person needing prayer as having no faith, defective faith, or think that the situation is "God's will" and therefore should just be accepted without praying for change. I think it's fair to say the apostle Paul had great faith, and yet he is pleading for people to "*fight alongside in prayer*" in Romans 15:30. To contend and battle in prayer for something is biblical, a privilege, and activates new realms of breakthrough and glory. Yet the benefits of contending are not always appreciated.

In the midst of the contending, remember you are loved completely. We press in because there's more, not because we need to earn "spiritual brownie points." Contending can look different in different seasons and moments, the point is that we continue in prayer.

I encourage you, as you contend, find joy, look for beauty, and seek childlike wonder. Living with childlike awe adds strength to our hearts as we contend. The enemy would have you hate contending and praying, and tell you it's the most boring thing you could do. This is just not the truth of prayer as Jesus taught us. Jesus' kind of prayer shifts Heaven to earth. That's exhilarating!

Decreeing from the throne room and pressing into the glory realm activates the manifest presence of God, *"Draw near to God and He will draw near to you"* (James 4:8 NKJV). Being in His manifest, tangible presence, where Heaven's atmosphere infuses you, is where the oil is multiplied and the fire on the altar of our hearts is stoked and becomes blazing hot. Then we burn, we become a burning-bush encounter, and contagious fire sparks off us to others. This is contending in prayer.

We don't "burn out" from praying, we burn out when we don't have oil as we pray. The wise virgins were called wise for a reason—they kept oil in reserve (see Matthew 25:1-13). We need the oil that comes from leaning into His presence. Apply oil liberally as you pray by spending time in His presence in worship, praise, and adoration. The oil keeps the fire burning.

I often say, and am going to say it again now—if we can have faith to catch a cold, then why can't we have faith to catch the fire of God! The fire of God is contagious, and we are all called to spread it around!

> *The fire must be kept burning on the altar continuously; it must not go out* (Leviticus 6:13).

The priests in the Old Testament were commanded to keep the fire burning on the altar at all times. *It must not go out!* We are a "royal priesthood" commanded to keep the fire burning on the altar of our hearts now. This isn't a good idea, it's a command of God. *The fire must not go out!*

Whatever we have to do, whatever we need to decree, whatever it costs. The fire in our hearts must not go out! We are destined to *burn* with a contagious fire after God. To do this we need to stoke the fire afresh every day. There's a contending and determination required to stay on fire and burn with a contagiousness that is caught by others.

The fire we carry is proportionate to the care we take to stoke the flames in our heart. There's a roar of intercession and sold out contending prayer arising around the world that will shift mountains, that is fueled from the oil of Heaven.

God is a consuming fire, and so I pray His consuming fire would spark an increasing, blazing fire in our hearts that burns ferociously and consumes everything that is unhelpful in our connection to Him. May God's fire activate new encounters and passion after Him. A fire is "alive." Its flames are perpetually moving and dancing, dynamic and animated. When we burn for God, we too feel alive, dynamic, filled with consuming, self-perpetuating passion. The on-fire you is the best version of you.

The fire of God is transferable, and it's the key to our next season. Lukewarm living will not open the doors reserved for the burning ones. Oh Lord, come and pour oil on the flames in our hearts. Come stir us to steward the fire within. Is there anything more worthy of our contending than to be a burning-bush encounter for others, and to burn with passion after the heart of our King.

Oh Lord, pour oil on the fire within us. Lord, make us walking, talking, mobile, transferable, perpetual burning flames of fiery love and passion after You so that everywhere we go, the fire of our God goes. Let people catch the fire, and contagious sparks fly everywhere our influence extends. This is our decree to contend for.

This is my life passion to burn with a contagious fire. I speak this over you, dear reader, in the name of Jesus. That you catch a spark of His consuming fire.

We are all called to be mobile, personal, contagious, revival fires. It is not a burden to contend for revival fire. It's an honor. To be a vessel that transports the oil of His presence, the consuming fire of God, the love of the Father, the hope of the nations, the atmosphere of Heaven, the answer to salvation—*this* is worthy of our lives. There is no other cause that matters more.

Being a fiery one is not a personality type. It's a decision to stay on the altar and become a surrendered living flame. The prayers of one who burns after the heart of Jesus calls down Elijah's fire and sees nations return to God. To contend for personal revival is to contend for national revival; because once tasted, we know everyone needs to experience how God's heart burns with love for them. Conviction, courage, and a yielded heart doesn't just set you on fire, it sets the world around you on fire.

I bless your soul to thrive in His fire as you contend to see the *"goodness of the Lord in the land of the living"* (Psalm 27:13 NKJV). The fire of God enables burning *as* we contend.

As we stand with each other and speak life, contending with fierce faith when required to *"fight alongside,"* this is answering Jesus' prayer, to pray and contend.

CONTENDING EXPLAINED

I understand the faith-and-hope battle of persevering faith and continued prayer in the middle of circumstances that are just *not good* and don't make sense. Sickness, injustice, and destructive circumstances are never from God, they are always from the devil. It's always God's heart and will for us to decree breakthrough. God's heart is always for the person, especially when things don't make sense. Knowing this helps in actual, *real* journeys of ups and downs.

Here's my simple explanation of why we continue to press in, even if it takes time, for something like healing, delayed breakthrough, new strategies, national reformation, and revival.

In the well-known Lord's Prayer, Jesus starts by saying, *"When you pray..."* and then gives instruction on things to do, and *not* do. Jesus is first of all assuming that we pray! He doesn't say *if* you pray, but *when* you pray. Then Jesus gives us a blueprint in Matthew 6:5-14 (NKJV) of *how* to pray, *when* we pray. Jesus says:

> *Our Father in heaven, hallowed be Your name. Your king-dom come. Your will be done on earth as it is in heaven....*

We learn a lot from this simple prayer format from Jesus that He gave us to use when we pray. First, Jesus is using the language of family, "our Father." We are family, and a heart connection to our heavenly Dad is the starting point. We haven't joined an organization or even an ideology or religion, we are part of a family.

Then Jesus says we are to honor God as we pray, *"Hallowed be Your name."* God is worthy, regardless of what we are pressing in for or dealing with. Next Jesus gives some of the most profound, yet simple wisdom on prayer and contending that answers pretty much all the questions that come up as we journey through life with God. Here goes:

JESUS' 101 OF CONTENDING

The Lord's Prayer tells us:

1. Jesus wants His Kingdom to come and His will to be done on earth as it is in Heaven.

2. Jesus is saying it is not yet like this.

3. Jesus wants us to pray and partner with Him to see God's will happen on earth by contending in prayer, as He asked us to do "when" we pray.

The end. Simple, isn't it.

Jesus' prayer here tells us that contending is essential to seeing earth's circumstances realigned fully to God's will. For instance, in Heaven there is no sickness and destruction, so we can pray with confidence that this is God's will and desire on the earth. Jesus is compelling us though, to grasp that our voice is part of the process, and our prayers are essential. What's more, our contending answers Jesus' prayer that we press in and pray like this. It equally tells us that it's possible and biblical to expect impossible circumstances to shift to "on earth as it is in Heaven" *as we pray*, and keep praying, until this is what we see.

It also says so simply—there is always hope! Jesus gave the solution, which is to pray and decree that Heaven's answers would infuse earth's circumstances. Jesus didn't say, "Well, just put up with it if something isn't aligned to His Word." No, Jesus said, *"Pray."* Pray because in My Father's house there are solutions.

This is what contending, like Jesus asked us to do, looks like. Contending, simply put, is persevering prayer. Contending is biblical. Contending is a request of Jesus. Contending acknowledges that stuff happens, but that our prayers our powerful and essential in releasing breakthrough. Most importantly, Jesus wants us, even commands us, to pray like this every time something doesn't align with God's heart and promises. Jesus wants us to pray more of Heaven into the earth, rather than just accepting things.

Bethel's Pastor Bill Johnson says, "Automatically thinking 'everything that happens is God's will' is a lazy way to live. We live in a war. Jesus wasn't fighting the Father's will when He raised the dead." This quote stirs me so much! We are called to release God's decrees from the throne room on earth. We are called to "fight alongside" each other and contend for "on earth as it is in Heaven."

I have some additional wisdom for you, friend, who is pressing in. Sometimes the most spiritual thing you can do in the midst of intense, persevering prayer, is go to bed and sleep. If you are physically exhausted, part of the solution to contending is sleep!

Likewise, sometimes contending can look like having fun as an act of defiant faith that we will not be shaken. Laughter, joy, enjoying God's presence, all these things are important and part of life-giving contending for the breakthrough. Seeing beauty around us while believing, soaking in God's presence to renew the oil, purposing to see gold, not just dirt. All of this sustains us as we contend, but it is also an act of warfare in and of itself. To laugh in the face of the enemy's lies is powerful. God sits in Heaven and laughs at His enemies (Psalm 2:4), and it's good for the soul for us to do the same.

I often take time for "fun" as warfare, especially when the battle is hot. It reminds me that God cares about my heart *during* the journey, and that taking care of my soul pleases the Lord. On the worst moments of the worst days, laughter is seriously good medicine (see Proverbs 17:22). It's another reason why I'm so blessed to have a husband who can find a way to laugh in the middle of storms—always!

Jesus wants us to thrive *as* we contend, and press in for ourselves and each other.

If someone is fighting a battle, and the battle is bigger than they are, that's our trumpet call to come gather and join our faith together and fight as a family! Yes, we are an army, but first we are a family. Jesus' prayer is a call to decree in unity and love, *"on earth as it is in Heaven."* It's our call to bless instead of curse, and stand together as family in faith and pray, contending as Jesus implored us to do.

Jesus' prayer is still echoing throughout the ages, *"When you pray, pray like this!"* Contend for each other, contend for your city, your nation, your family, your call, and your circumstances. Jesus' prayer was not a call to shoot the wounded. It was an announcement as much a prayer, that we are empowered to change the earth with our decrees and persevering prayer. All Heaven agrees. May our voice be found agreeing with Jesus as well—on earth as it is in our Father's Home.

I am convinced that as we join our faith together and contend together in the unity of Kingdom family, we are going to see unprecedented greater glory. The harvest in my own backyard and sphere of influence is ready now. Unheard-of-before miracles await our contending, ground-breaking breakthroughs never before experienced will increasingly cover the earth as we answer Jesus' prayer, and *pray!*

Jesus wants, implores, asks, desires, calls, showed us, and commands us to *contend*. This is the King's decree. When you pray, pray like this—contend. There is more in Heaven available for earth than we've seen, and our prayers are unleashing increasing breakthroughs in our lifetime.

THE KING'S DECREE FOR YOU

"My child, I am inviting you to partner with Me in what I am doing on the earth. Persevere in prayer because your prayers shift the atmosphere. Your contending impacts the world around you and is changing more than you see. I am with you; I am proud of you: keep moving forward."

—THE KING

MY PRAYER FOR YOU

I pray fresh, supernatural strength over you as you courageously persevere and stand in faith. I also decree that the very atmosphere of Heaven would infuse your thinking right now. I decree that delay is breaking and new beginnings are breaking through, as the God of the breakthrough roars over your life. I'm blessing your faith with supernatural strength, and calling in sweet victories and unusual favor.

You're loved and celebrated, and I ask for a noticeable shift of favor that releases new harvest and breakthroughs. I ask God for fresh revelation that reveals to you how deeply God adores you, that He is completely for you and championing you into destiny. I pray that you encounter aspects of God's glory and beauty that cause your heart to soar, and contend with new passion and joy. In Jesus' name, amen.

DECREE

- I am contagious with the fire of God. It is easy to catch, and I will spread it everywhere I go.

- I am a walking, talking, mobile, revival fire.

- I contend and persevere in prayer for God's will to be done on earth as it is in Heaven.

- I am an answer to the prayer of Jesus when I pray and decree "Your will be done on earth as it is in Heaven."

Chapter 8

Now Faith Is for Now

*Now faith is confidence in what we hope for
and assurance about what we do not see.*
—Hebrews 11:1

God is releasing "now faith" to the body of Christ. *Now* faith is the essential ingredient for this season of greater glory and breakthrough. The first two words of Hebrews 11:1 are, *"Now faith"*! Without now faith, we can miss what is available *now*. The harvest is won, breakthrough is activated, and revival is released by those with now faith for our current circumstances to be shifted by God's power, *now!* I understand that this is a play on words; however, the truth remains the same, faith is for now.

Now faith is crucial for breakthrough as it empowers us to believe for the more that is required for actually breaking through.

Without now faith, we will never steward our current generation, and we will delay action, always attaching our faith to a season "four months away" (John 4:35 TPT) and a future, undetermined time. This leaves "now" devoid of hope instead of saturated in hope that God wants to move right *now*. Hebrews 11:1 is cheering on faith for *now!*

Now read the first *four* words of Hebrews 11:1. Oh how I love this verse! *"Now faith is confidence...."* Let me put it this way, now faith gives us confidence that God is moving right now in "that" situation we are facing. Without confidence that God is moving now, why would we pray? Confident expectation comes from now faith. Without confident expectation for now, and a belief that our intercession and decrees actually partner with Heaven and change things as we release them, our prayer is hindered. Now faith imparts confidence that nothing we are facing is devoid of hope or without God's redemption; therefore, it gives us confident hope that effects how we pray. We need now faith.

Leaning into the verse even more, *"Now faith is confidence in what we hope for and assurance about what we do not see."* Not only does now faith impact our hope levels and how we pray, it also assures us that even when we haven't seen the fullness of what we are believing for yet, we can trust that God is completing what He began. Did you get that? *Now faith assures us* that even when we don't see *yet,* we can trust God.

This is life changing. This verse says that now faith confidently believes for what we haven't seen yet. So let me encourage you, if you are still believing for the fullness of a promise that is in process, you are not without faith, you are walking in now faith that is current, active, and confident. This truth is imperative to hold on to, for if our faith can only thrive where we have seen the fullness of breakthrough, shame or disappointment will try and cause us to give up. A journey that takes time doesn't disqualify faith. Road-tested faith is renewable and remains active in the moments we don't see yet. This is now faith that is real, preserving, and can be applied every day and in every situation in our current world.

Now faith is the crucial ingredient in those who see increasing glory, miracles, and breakthrough as they persevere—and just don't quit.

How to Increase Now Faith

So then faith comes by hearing, and hearing by the word of God (Romans 10:17 NKJV).

There is a truth that is often overlooked in this verse about faith as we sometimes hear it and dismiss it as "religious thinking." Faith comes from hearing! We can grow our faith by speaking out the Word of God. Once again, *our own voice* is part of the solution. The simple act of decreeing truth literally activates and increases faith. Our voice is powerful, and speaking out God's Word and what God is saying for our own ears to hear, increases faith! Our own voice becomes a faith activator; and as we speak, faith rises. No wonder the devil has wanted to silence you! You are a faith activator!

It's so easy for these things to become lifeless, religious procedures instead of life-giving keys to breakthrough. It's not about a lifeless process, it's about stirring our faith so we are positioned for more. Speaking out God's Word, and letting our soul hear truth, cancels out the voice of the devil and activates that "something" inside us that responds to the voice of Heaven.

It doesn't have to be hard, or fancy. For instance, for over a decade almost every single time I get up to minister, publicly or privately, I decree out loud to myself, "I'm nothing without You, Lord, but with You I can do all things" (Philippians 4:13). I have prayed it so many times that as soon as I say it now, my faith is activated for "all things." It's not a fancy prayer, but it speaks, and it always activates anointing and faith in me.

It's Not About How, but Who

God wants to take His people places we have not been before, so solidifying our faith in Him "for what we do not see," is so important. When we look at the bigness of the prophetic Promised Land God is stirring us to take new territory in, it's normal to ask, "But how, God?" Of course *how* is important, but far more important is *who*. *Whose* hand are we holding as we step into the unknown? Who is our trust in? Whose voice are we following? Has God spoken, and have we listened and obeyed? When our faith is in God, our *how* surrenders to *who*.

India Through Mum's Eyes

"Go to India now," I heard God say years ago. There was an urgency to it. I had astoundingly never been to India in all the years my parents were missionaries there. I had put off going for many reasons, somewhat because it was a lot of money for our entire family to go, but mostly because living with intestinal problems and the health challenges associated with that, going to India wasn't the easiest or most fun of places to think about going!

But I knew I heard God. God was activating faith that superseded my fears. Ben had been there before and agreed it was time for us all to go. So our family went off on an epic adventure to India for a month of ministry with my Mum and Dad who were missionaries there for 20-plus years.

I had one prayer before leaving that you may find funny, but I asked God to provide Western toilets for me. I'm being very honest with you—I understood this was a big ask, but at the time it seemed so important. It was incredible how God answered this very personal prayer for our entire trip. Anyone who's been to India and away from major hotels knows this answer to my prayer was miraculous to say the least! God is so kind and amazing.

We had the most amazing time in India—powerful ministry, notable miracles, and many salvations. We watched scars disappear from wounds before our eyes, blind eyes open, tumors disappear, instant deliverance, and many people finding freedom. It was glorious. Truly India was, and is, an incredible nation I fell in love with.

These precious moments just being with Mum and Dad and seeing all they had pioneered there were priceless. Meeting all their friends and family who loved them so dearly in India was incredible. I got to meet the people I had only heard about in stories, and I cried many tears as India got in my blood and made me a better person. Since then, India has become a nation we have ongoing love for and connection to. To see India through my Mum and Dad's eyes and what caused them to give their lives to this nation was deeply impactful.

I am blessed my parents always stretched my faith growing up. In India, when something broke, it wasn't easy to replace things. Dad would pray resurrection over appliances all the time, and so it was normal to hear testimonies of fridges, TVs and toasters "coming back to life." My Dad prayed these kind of prayers long before they went to India actually, and I remember wild miracles like this happening often as I grew up.

I just have to tell you one of my favorite miracles I saw as a teenager because it built "wild faith" in me. Our family car had stopped working, apparently the battery had died. Dad got the jumper cables out to charge the battery. He attached them to our car and suddenly realized that wouldn't work, as there was no other car to attach the cables to—funny, I know! Well, true to form, I watched Dad hold the cables in the air as if to plug them into "Heaven" and he shouted out loud, "POWER!" Immediately, the battery revved and the car started running! I couldn't believe my eyes! God had started the car at Dad's decree! Wow, God. And thanks, Dad, for building *wild* faith in me.

When we said goodbye to my parents at the train station as we left for the long seventeen-hour train ride back to the airport, I wept my heart out. I remember hugging Mum and not wanting to let go. I was used to them being away, so goodbyes weren't uncommon. This response wasn't normal for me, but I couldn't stop crying. I cried almost the entire train ride, and for days after. My heart ached in a way I couldn't explain.

Five months later, we had to unexpectedly fly my Mum home to Australia with an urgent medical need, and she sadly went to Heaven five days later. That goodbye at the train station when my Mum was in good health and in her element of all she was called to do, suddenly took on deeper meaning and preciousness. How thankful I am that God said, "Go to India now." How kind God was to give us that precious time together. How thankful I am that we listened and obeyed. I can't tell you how thankful I am for that month in India.

Faith Is Not a Feeling, It's Obedience

While it's true that faith is often accompanied with a feeling, faith is not first a feeling! If we wait for a "feeling" of faith to hit us before speaking truth or obeying God, we can be waiting a long time. Faith is ultimately an act of obedience to the truth of His Word—feelings are secondary. I didn't say feelings aren't important, as they are, just not as important as obeying.

To have faith in God is a decision to believe and trust God. I want to encourage you, friend, feelings can deceive us. You can "feel" nothing, and yet activate faith and see miracles flow. I've often prayed for people "by faith" when not "feeling" very bold, and I've seen amazing miracles happen, which is always humbling. Ultimately, this reminds us it's not us, it's Him, always! The enemy wants to tell you that you have little or no faith because you don't "*feel*" full of faith. Tell the devil to take a hike in Jesus' name. Faith is not a feeling, it's obedience.

While on I'm talking about this topic, I know there are those whose hearts will soak in this truth right now. You are loved by God, even when you don't feel anything! God's love of you is not dependent on if you can feel it! Experiencing God's love *is* available, important, and for you to "experience," but God's love for you is not dependent on you feeling it for it to be truth. You are loved fully and completely, end of story. Say to yourself, "I am loved even when I don't feel a thing." God says in Jeremiah 31:3 about you: *"I have loved you with an everlasting love; I have drawn you with unfailing kindness."*

FAITH GROWS WHEN YOU EXERCISE IT

I like to think of faith just like a muscle. And just like any other muscle in our body, our faith muscle gets stronger when we exercise it. As we step out, activate, and use our faith, it grows! As we trust God with what we have, increase comes. We can all do that, even those of us who might say we have little faith, that's great, use what you have, and more grows. We may not feel full of faith right now, but as we activate *the faith of God* right now and say that *the same spirit that rose Jesus from dead lives in me* (read Romans 8:11), we activate this same faith in us. I ask for this to be released in you right now! Remember, mustard-seed faith is powerful (Luke 17:6).

Tell God, "I trust You to grow faith in me, but I refuse to believe that feelings of little faith disqualify me from walking in great faith. I trust You, God, and Your Word. If you said it, I believe it."

NOW FAITH SHIFTS NOW CHALLENGES

Now faith, put simply, is faith for now! It's present faith, or activated faith, that attaches itself to the challenges you are facing now and believes for a shift right now. This is the kind of faith that the world needs right now. God is releasing new realms of now faith into the body for unprecedented miracles, signs and wonders, and mass evangelism. There's a courage coming on the voice of the Church that is shifting Heaven to earth in every realm of society.

Now faith is the secret ingredient of decreeing to the impossible. Now faith is the foundation needed to activate breakthrough. Now faith stirs hope and causes us to press in decreeing God's promises over situations where giants are trying to squash, intimidate, and control you.

Now Faith Believes We Can Achieve

Now faith believes that we can rise above whatever has come against us and any obstacle that stands in the way of promise. Now faith believes we can achieve what God has promised and whispered to our hearts, even things that seem difficult. It stirs us to believe what God says about us and take steps to advance into increase. Something begins to stir in us when God is increasing our faith. We look at mountains differently; instead of thinking that it can't be done, our spirit soars with expectation that we are about to be part of a miracle that will define our season.

When faith is rising, we look at obstacles surrounding us and instead of seeing just roadblocks, we see the vastness of the army of the Lord surrounding us and urging us forward. Courage arises and we become the best version of ourselves. Without our faith attached to what God is stirring in us for ourselves, our families and nations, we are paralyzed in inaction. Now faith mobilizes not just hope, but action.

A recalibration is taking place in our hearts across the body as a whole, as a divine plumb line is reestablished. God is calling us back to the simpleness of the raw and real Gospel. Healthy fear of the Lord is recalibrating hearts with the holiness of God and urgency of winning souls. We are being marked with His consuming fire; and a childlike faith that trusts in the face of insurmountable odds looks like picking up stones to throw at Goliaths. Because God did it before, He will do it again, my friend. God is tenderly reminding us that we don't outgrow, or mature beyond, the need to trust and obey.

God can be trusted where He is leading us, as He is upgrading us to extend the borders of our faith. Initially though as the past season's wineskin is removed, it can feel more like loss than an upgrade. Hold tight, the new wineskin is worth the sense of displacement, as God is making room in our hearts for the *new*.

Now Faith Believes for Now Harvest

Jesus spoke out to the people in John 4:35, *"Don't you have a saying, 'It's still four months until harvest'? I tell you, open your eyes and look at the fields! They're ripe for harvest."*

The Passion Translation says it this way, *"As the crowds emerged from the village, Jesus said to his disciples, 'Why would you say, "The harvest is another four months away"? Look at all the people coming— now is harvest time! For their hearts are like vast fields of ripened grain—ready for a spiritual harvest'"* (John 4:35 TPT).

Oh this verse stirs me! Why indeed would we say the harvest is still four months away when God is doing something right now! There is fresh oil on this verse at the moment. God is stirring in our hearts faith for our now. As prophetic people, we notoriously put all our faith expectations into a distant season, and carry little faith for what God is actually doing right now. Yes, our decrees establish tomorrow, but they also establish now!

We are called to steward the season we are in right now. We are each called to steward our current time we live in, our current circumstances, and to stir and carry faith for God to move right now. God has harvest and breakthrough reserved for our now season. Why would we put all our faith in what God can do tomorrow and reserve little faith for what God can do now? The new breed that is arising has faith to impact this generation and win a now harvest.

I'm aware Jesus is talking about a harvest of souls in John 4:35, but I extend my faith to believe that "harvest" is also fruitfulness from seeds sown. God has a harvest of breakthroughs marked for you right now as you activate your faith.

It's faith for now that God is restoring back to the body so that we purposefully steward this season and this generation. The generation alive now desperately needs Jesus, and a Church that is on fire. Let's ask ourselves:

- If we don't steward this generation and this season, who will?
- If our voices don't speak to the current climate of fear, whose will?
- If our decrees don't activate faith for restored justice, whose will?
- If our hearts don't have courage to take down the giants of our culture, whose will?
- If our faith doesn't believe for unprecedented revival, souls saved, and miracles, whose will?

We can't afford to attach all our faith to another season, another people, and another time as this is the season in which we are alive and *now* is the time of harvest.

We hold the ear of the King, and we are His mouthpiece on the earth right now. We are indeed in a royal position of authority for such a time as *now!*

> *For if you remain silent at this time, relief and deliverance for the Jews will arise from another place, but you*

and your father's family will perish. And who knows but that you have come to your royal position for such a time as this? (Esther 4:14)

Now faith brings our hopes into reality and challenges us to believe for more and be stirred for miracles in our everyday current circumstances regardless of what we have seen or haven't seen so far. Now faith doesn't put off believing for increased breakthrough until another day or another generation, it takes ownership of *now*.

God is stirring us to activate the truth that faith that shifts mountains, takes out giants, and raises Lazarus situations from the grave is still available today. This kind of faith is accessed through our own voice, obedience, and action.

TRUST AND OBEY ENCOUNTER

A few months ago, I had a dream where I was hearing the old hymn, "Trust and Obey." As I woke up, I was singing this song, and at the same time I heard an angel next to me singing it too. The angel was singing so beautifully. You may remember this hymn. I remembered it from growing up in the Salvation Army, but had not heard it for a long time. The lyrics include: "Trust and obey, for there's no other way, to be happy in Jesus, than to trust and obey." The words are so simple and true. The song got *stuck* in my head, and I knew God was speaking.

I researched a little and discovered that this hymn was written in 1886, inspired by a testimony at the well-known revival meetings with Dwight L. Moody in Brockton, Massachusetts. A man there was so touched by what God was doing as revival fire stirred his heart, he stood and shared a testimony saying, "I am not quite sure—but I am going to trust, and I am going to obey." It clearly resonated with the hearts of a generation who weren't sure about a lot of things, but knew God was calling them back to His heart and the simple message of " trust and obey." This hymn was based on the man's testimony, put to music, and it went around the world igniting faith and became an anthem for that generation and beyond.

I knew that through this hymn was God emphasizing a point as can only happen when God organizes something. We were driving to Massachusetts and preaching that night only a few miles from where the revival took place and the song was written. It also happened to be my first time back to that part of the country in eight years. I believe God is stirring the wells of revival all over again! I understood God was saying that to *trust and obey* wasn't just a great old hymn, it was key to this next season of revival. God was touching the hearts of the harvesters themselves, reminding us of the simpleness of the gospel, and inviting us to say afresh, "I will trust and obey."

Heaven is restoring now faith and consecrating our hearts to the simple, timeless message of trust and obey. This hymn was amplified across the nations because it called people back to simple faith. God is doing this again in our day. As God released this song over 100 years ago, multitudes of souls came into the Kingdom as awakening reaped a harvest. God is ready to do the same again. Are we?

I'm including the words of the old hymn here. They are words from another era, but they still speak and are alive today. Let this be your prayer.

TRUST AND OBEY

When we walk with the Lord
in the light of His word,
what a glory He sheds on our way!
While we do His good will,
He abides with us still,
and with all who will trust and obey.
(Refrain)
Trust and obey, for there's no other way
to be happy in Jesus, but to trust and obey.
Not a burden we bear,
not a sorrow we share,
but our toil He doth richly repay;
not a grief or a loss,
not a frown or a cross,
but is blest if we trust and obey.
But we never can prove
the delights of His love
until all on the altar we lay;
for the favor He shows,
for the joy He bestows,
are for them who will trust and obey.
Then in fellowship sweet
we will sit at His feet,
or we'll walk by His side in the way;
what He says we will do,
where He sends we will go;
never fear,
only trust and obey.
Trust and obey, for there's no other way

to be happy in Jesus, but to trust and obey.
(Hymn writer: John H. Sammis, 1846–1919)

THE KING'S DECREE FOR YOU

"My child, keep believing, stay full of hope, stay full of faith.
Be confident in what I have spoken. Faith is for today
as much as it is for tomorrow. I am releasing now faith."
—THE KING

MY PRAYER FOR YOU

My prayer for you right now is that you know God is with
you, faithful one. I speak a fresh, deep connection of your
heart to Jesus and childlike faith to trust and obey. Your
heart is precious to Father God, and He is leading you
into more than you've experienced before and extending
the borders of your faith to add blessing to you. Let your
expectations rise and your hope burst forth, because King
Jesus is with you, mighty one.

Your prayers are shifting impossible to possible in your life.
I'm blessing your faith and I call you a faith catalyst for
miracles that release Heaven's heart everywhere you go.
Keep going courageous friend, because what you carry is
unique and needed in this season.

I pray for you surprise kindnesses of God this week that
melt your heart and show you just how precious you are to
Him. I'm asking the Lord to give you encounters that stir

and stretch what you are believing for, and release peace that God is right here with you every step of the way. I pray the awe of God stirs new childlike trust and security in your heart. Be blessed, faithful warrior, in Jesus' name, amen.

DECREE

- I decree that I walk in faith for the now—and faith for the not yet.

- Faith is not defined by my feelings. I have faith for now. Faith is my obedience to what God has decreed.

- I will trust and obey my heavenly Father.

- The harvest is now, not four months off. I decree my time is now for a fruitful harvest of breakthroughs in my life and souls for the Kingdom.

- I am never alone. God is always with me.

Chapter 9

PROCESS IS NOT YOUR ENEMY

You keep every promise you've ever made to me! Since
your love for me is constant and endless, I ask you, Lord,
to finish every good thing that you've begun in Me!
—Psalm 138:8 TPT

Process is not the evil cousin of promise. Process is the pathway to promise and there rarely is a promise that doesn't have a process to walk through. If we say yes to the promise, we are in fact, saying yes to the process.

We all go through process in our journey with God—you may be going through a *process* right now. In this chapter I speak to those who are walking through a process even as you read this. Before I start though, it's really important to qualify what I'm about to say, as make no mistake, anyone on a journey is not *condemned* to a lengthy, unending process. God *is* the God of breakthrough (read 2 Samuel 5:20) and the God of healing, miracles, and solutions *now*! Now faith is for now, and this is my prayer for you—breakthrough now. However, at times there is a process to walk through, and this chapter speaks directly to that journey.

I want to assure you that God is not withholding His promises from you or delaying your thriving. There is a way to thrive in your soul even during *process*. God doesn't give a promise and then stand back and say, "Only when you reach the destination will I exchange beauty for ashes and joy of the Lord for despair."

Neither does God separate Himself from us when we walk through process. He is with us on the good days, the hard days, and days in-between as we pursue the manifestation of the fullness of promises in our lives and circumstances. God's presence, is present—*always*.

He also doesn't punish us with a process that we cannot overcome with His grace and thrive in our soul in the midst of real life. I'm not for a moment saying that process isn't challenging, but I am saying God is in the process with us.

Please hear my cheering you on. Having been through the normal ups and downs of ministry, life, family, and health challenges, particularly over the past thirty years, I say this with confidence. No process is void of God's presence, hope, and supernatural strengthening to keep going. Every process is a pathway into the destiny God has spoken for you. God has never left me on the worst days or in the worst moments; in fact, He's drawn even closer. I pray His closeness over you, too.

When challenges seem unending, this is the moment to remind ourselves that process, or transition as it's otherwise called, is taking us into the very thing we have been asking God for. It's healthy to cast off some lies and distorted truths the enemy wants to tell us when walking through a process into promise.

God has shown me so many nuggets about process that I want to list a few. As you read them, take note of what speaks loudly to you:

- Process is not your enemy.
- You can thrive in any season, including the journey to God's promise.
- You can be productive in process.
- A miracle in process is not failure—it's a miracle unfolding.
- Your circumstances are *not* your identity.
- Shame and condemnation are *not* from God, *ever.*
- You have bold faith if you are believing for more than you've seen yet.
- A season, even a long one, always ends—and a new season begins.
- What God begins, He completes, *always.*
- We can capture a promise in our spirit before it manifests in the natural.
- There is grace for the race, not just the finish.
- Any promise is made up of a mix of process, faithfulness, perseverance, acceleration, and suddenlies.
- God remembers His promises to you.
- When you have no words left, God translates your tears as prayer.
- Flourishing is not reserved just for when breakthrough comes.

- Promises are exactly that, and you can trust the promise Giver.
- God calls you an overcomer.
- God is the God of breakthrough, and He is breaking through for you. It's one of the very names given to Him by David, *"Baal Perazim";* in Hebrew it literally means "God of the breakthrough" (see 2 Samuel 5:20).

If any of those points resonated or stirred you a little, take a moment and ask the Lord to minister upgraded truth. I want to encourage you, friend, that God is breaking through and finishing every good thing He has begun in your life. *Every* good thing He's begun! All those half-finished stories He began will be completed with His redemptive power. Even the stories that seem to have been interrupted, taken forever to write, or the enemy interrupted the flow, God is completing them all.

You Are a Faith Hero

Now faith is confidence in what we hope for and assurance about what we do not see (Hebrews 11:1).

My friend, receive this truth that you are a faith hero from the heart of Heaven right now. You are a Kingdom faith hero! You who are walking through circumstances that are painful, challenging, and out of alignment with what God has promised, and yet you are still believing. You are still believing in the midst of incomplete promise and fullness of all God has spoken—*you*, yes you are a Kingdom faith hero. I honor your courageous faith.

The enemy wants you to think you don't have faith because you haven't seen "it" fully yet. The opposite is actually true. You *do* have faith because you continue to believe when you have not seen yet. Hebrews 11:1 defines faith as being assured of what we do not see, which gives us confidence as we contend, pray, and believe.

Just because you have not seen the fullness yet or haven't seen the completed breakthrough yet manifested, does not mean you do not have faith. Faith isn't required for what has already happened! Be encouraged, friend, you who has fought to hold on to faith in the midst of raging attacks from the enemy and an onslaught of enemy fire—*you* are a Kingdom hero who walks in Hebrews 11 faith!

You have bold faith, courageous one, who will receive great reward. The Passion Translation says, *"So don't lose your bold, courageous faith, for you are destined for a great reward!"* (Hebrews 10:35).

I speak honor over you, my friend. Honor for pushing through, persevering, holding on and believing God for where you have seen *and* for where you haven't seen yet. You have bold faith, and all of Heaven is applauding your strength as you ignore the enemy's lies. You have shown fierce faith to stand on truth in the midst of seemingly unending, drawn-out battle. I want you to hear God say, "Well done, good and faithful warrior." Heaven is honoring your bold faith. The King is honoring *you.*

SHAME AND CONDEMNATION ARE *NEVER* FROM GOD

I break off anything that has come at you to heap shame on you as you walk *"through the valley of the shadow"* (Psalm 23:4 NKJV) into greater freedom and increased breakthrough. Those little jabs of critical words or throw-away comments intended to heap shame on you are not from God. Neither are the condemning lies and thoughts that say you are unworthy while on the pathway of process and progress toward breakthrough and increasing miracles. I tell all this to be broken off your life and removed from affecting your identity, in Jesus' name.

God upgrades our character and deals with sin or unhealthy thinking processes as we journey if there are areas in us that need an upgrade of Kingdom purity. Don't make this process bigger than it needs to be. Just simply repent of sin, receive forgiveness, and move on free. Remember, when God reveals, it's always to heal.

> Yet **in all these things** we are more than **conquerors** through Him who loved us (Romans 8:37 NKJV).

Through the power of the Holy Spirit, we have power to overcome and conquer *"all these things."* I often speak over myself, "I am an overcomer. I am more than a conqueror." So are you through Jesus. If you love Jesus, this is your identity, *"more than a conqueror,"* and so we are empowered to overcome in "all these things."

To say it another way, if you are in the middle of a battle and persevering, you are an overcomer and called a conqueror. Conquerors, conquer. Overcomers, overcome. The decree of the King is speaking overcoming power over you right now in the midst of the battle. Romans 8:37 is calling you a champion who is designed to overcome every challenge you face.

I'm far from a Greek expert, but I just love this, so let me try and explain this simply. The word "conqueror" in Romans 8:37, according to the Strong's Concordance, originates from the Greek word *hupernikao*. Forget about trying to say it! But get this, *hupernikao* implies an overcomer; a champion, a victor, "to vanquish and gain a decisive victory"! This is in your DNA to rise above and gain decisive victory through Jesus.

Knowing we are designed for decisive victory impacts how we think about ourselves. This is especially important when we're in the heat of the battle. The battle doesn't define us, or prophesy to us. God defines us and prophesies decisive victories. This is who we are. This is who *you* are. A champion of faith, in the process of walking into increasing victory. You are made to overcome and you already are an overcomer in "all these things" as you proceed in faith, believing for what you haven't seen yet! If you are in process and persevering, you have bold faith.

Capture a Miracle in Your Spirit

You may need to hear this—a miracle in process is not a failure, it's a miracle unfolding. Every time you pray in faith, and then you pray again, you are contending, and *progressing*. You are shifting Heaven to earth, as you partner with faith. The act of believing when you haven't fully seen is the recipe for miracles.

When we let the truth of God's Word and the atmosphere of the glory realm infuse our hearts, we "capture" a miracle in our spirits long before we see it fully manifest on earth. When we marinate in truth and in the atmosphere of "possible," faith rises up inside us. The miracle becomes "real" in us *before* we ever see it with our eyes. This is capturing a miracle in your spirit!

Then from this place we stand, we decree, we believe until we see. And yet in His glory, in the atmosphere of His manifest presence, we have already received what His Word has promised. The time in-between manifestation and promise received by faith, is one expression of the working of miracles and often looks like *process and progress.*

Not every miracle is instant, but every prayer of faith is heard by God and affecting change (read 1 John 5:14-15). That's key. Did you catch that? Not every miracle is instant. Some miracles unfold with process. A miracle unfolding, is equally a miracle. And remember, you are not condemned to unending process. Many miracles are suddenlies. God is the God of breakthrough—and He is breaking through even when it has taken time.

Don't Quit the Process

In the midst of process the enemy will try and tell you to quit. He knows that *this* pathway leads to taking new ground and displacing giants. The only recourse the enemy has is to heap discouragement and shame on you, tell you the journey isn't worth it, or that you're a failure and you will never overcome. Sound familiar?

Hold on in these moments, victorious one. Hold on, bold warrior of faith. Your faith is shifting circumstances and changing history; even now while you are in the middle of your very own miracle, Heaven is cheering your faith.

I say to you, "You're not going backward. Your decrees are taking ground." May you hear this in the deepest places, like deep calling out to deep, "You are not going backward, you are advancing. You are taking ground." Every time you just get up and believe when all hell wants you to give up, every time you say, "I trust you God where I do not see," every time you stand and say, "I see the mountains becoming level ground," *every single time* you keep going and decree truth, your faith is taking ground in the spirit. And taking ground in the spirit is how we take ground in the natural.

You are stronger than you think and fiercer than the devil wants you to know. Your breakthrough is closer than the devil wants you to think. The demonic realm shudders when you stand to decree, because in *you,* God has found one who will believe where you cannot yet see! *This is powerful!* And I hear the Lord saying, "You will see, you will see, you will see." The heavens are opening and the rain of supernatural refreshing and restoration, healing and resurrection power are coming.

SUPERNATURAL RAIN IS FALLING

As I write this, I can feel supernatural rain on my arm and my leg—it feels just like soft, refreshing rain. It's beginning to rain, my friend. It's beginning to rain where there has been only drought. The "pent-up flood" of breakthrough is breaking through the resistance.

> *For he will come like a pent-up flood that the breath of the Lord drives along* (Isaiah 59:19).

God's very breath is driving along a pent-up flood of promises and indeed revival. It will come like a flood, like a rushing of waters, like a glorious sudden shift of divine change, and *His breath* is driving it along. God's breath is the force behind your breakthrough, and the force behind this next great awakening that will astound the nations. Nothing can stand in its way; no demon, no stronghold, no lie, no weapon formed against you, no adversary, no impossible mountain can hold back what God has prepared for you and me. The resistance is breaking, the pent-up flood is coming. I speak forth rain, rain, rain from the atmosphere of Heaven over you. The heavens are opening, the pent-up flood is breaking.

SUPERNATURAL RAIN MIRACLES

Supernatural rain has been a sign and wonder that has followed our ministry, and personally really encouraged me in many ways. To us it is a sign of revival rain, refreshing, and breakthrough. *"For there is the sound of a heavy rain"* (1 Kings 18:41). Some translations say, *"abundance of rain."* I can still feel supernatural rain as I write this, so I'm believing for miracles as you read this!

I have prophesied, "I hear the sound of heavy rain…" so many times I've lost count, but many times with supernatural rain falling on me. We are not prophesying into the distant future anymore, we are prophesying into the *now*. I speak forth this new sound of heavy rain and breakthrough over you now, in Jesus' name.

Years ago, we were driving home from a particularly glory-filled meeting one night on the Gold Coast of Australia, and it started to physically rain inside our car! There were no holes in our roof and it wasn't raining outside. Yes, both Ben and I felt it, saw it, and touched real rain drops on us. I tell you, that stretched my faith to believe for even more and different creative miracles.

Many times, suddenly as I've prayed for people, raindrops have dripped down on them and me, and often healing began to manifest. I remember one man in outback Australia who drove more than four hours to the meeting and needed his shoulder healed. A huge drop of water fell on my arm—although we were indoors—as I prayed, and it splashed over us both. Instantly the pain left his shoulder as Jesus healed him.

Another time I was praying for a man who really needed significant breakthrough and we both saw in the spirit at the same time supernatural lightning come over my right shoulder and suddenly hit him. He instantly fell to the ground as though dead. I must admit, I wondered if he was. Later he got up completely delivered and a different man.

It was very interesting that when the lightning from Heaven hit, I had my eyes closed, and for a while I could see with x-ray vision, that's the only way I can describe it. My eyes were shut but I could see everything in the room, front and back, in an x-ray kind of way. God's power adds clarity of vision to us in His glory.

Many times in meetings people have heard rain or thunder or felt rain and winds. Just recently at a church in Lindale, Texas, we released a prophetic word about revival rain and harvest. Afterward at a church prayer meeting, *everyone* in the room heard heavy rain falling on the church roof. They were all shocked when they walked outside and the ground was completely dry, there were clear skies and no sign of rain!

During the Pineapple Revival, many times people felt rain or we could see it falling in the air in front of us as we prayed inside the building. One time during our pre-service prayer, I started feeling supernatural rain and looked up and could see heavy rain falling on top of us inside the building. It felt like regular rain, yet no water! I asked who else could see it. Nearly everyone in the prayer meeting could either see it or feel it, including the guest speaker, a well-respected international prophet. It was fun actually, and represented God pouring out His manifest presence—which let me tell you, He did that night!

HEALING REVIVING RAIN

While we were traveling as a family all over outback Australia releasing revival, we would feel and see rain in our car many times. As I was still in the process of ongoing healing in my body, some days were harder than others physically. Sometimes when we would arrive at a town and our meeting was to begin in a few hours I'd feel so sick I couldn't get off the bed where we were staying. I would think, *There's no way I can minister tonight, Lord, I can't even get out of bed.* And so often, in fact almost every time in that season, supernatural rain would start to fall on me as I lay on the bed. I knew it was God. I never took it for granted, and it *always* brought out childlike joy in me and it revived me!

A process of physical strengthening and healing was taking place supernaturally in the glory that felt like rain. Sometimes I felt great, other times just well enough to get up and minister, but always things changed in His manifest presence. I was experiencing a supernatural process taking place. Doctors knew we traveled, and when I would have scheduled checkups, often they would say, "Whatever you're doing, keep doing it!" I'd laugh as I'd think of trying to explain to them exactly what was happening!

These were some of the best days of my life. I've had a lot of those best days; actually, I still am in the best days of my life!

Were there hard moments? Absolutely! But what I know is, by God's grace my soul was truly thriving in that season, and it was transforming my body from the inside out.

Sometimes when I am sitting in our prayer room I feel tiny drops of rain start to fall like a light sun shower. Other times I can be decreeing revival and feel big, heavy raindrops.

My favorite supernatural rain stories are seeing people's reactions when they realize that what they've heard about, and perhaps even doubted God would do, starts happening to them. God loves to mess with our measure of faith and expand it for more.

Just a couple of months ago we were ministering at a church in New England and one-third of the people felt supernatural rain.

Immediately faith broke into the room for revival in the United States, and miracles in *their* lives.

One of the amazing things these supernatural rain miracles have done in my life is grown me and literally shown me that the glory realm is far more real than the natural realm! It's not about the rain though, as much as it is a glorious sign and wonder that has blessed me, it's about Jesus reminding us He's big! I love that! Nothing is impossible for Him (Luke 1:37). Rain, feathers, gold dust, angelic encounters, healing, miracles—it's all about Jesus! Sometimes God is just reminding us He is still the God of all things are possible. Signs point to something, Jesus.

Every promise, every testimony, every manifestation of His glory along the journey is intended to build our faith. Our awe and wonder of just how incredible and powerful our King Jesus really is, is expanded as we look to see Jesus hidden in plain view in the processes of life. Everything is about Jesus.

THE POWER OF PROGRESS AND PROCESS

Slowly, day by day, I learned the power of celebrating progress and process, and blessing what God had begun while remaining engaged in faith for more. Thankfulness is powerful, especially as we celebrate the small beginnings.

You may not experience supernatural rain—though many do when we start talking about it—but you will have a testimony of how God has encouraged you. Embrace your testimonies, big and small, and all you have to be thankful for. Celebrate your progress, every step forward, no matter how small, it is worthy of praise. Use your testimonies as weapons to strike the ground in the process of decreeing more.

Bless the process God is using to fulfill His promises to you. Bless what God is unfolding in your life as what God orchestrates is always fruitful and filled with possibility. God doesn't take you on dead-end journeys. God's pathways lead to life and increase. And know this, you are walking into more and more because God completes every good work He begins. The small beginnings in your life are as blessed as the huge suddenlies. I bless you with more!

THE KING'S DECREE FOR YOU

"I keep every promise I have made to you. I do not lie, every word is true and every promise is faithful. My love for you is constant and I am finishing everything I have started. Keep trusting and keep holding My hand as we walk together."
—THE KING

MY PRAYER FOR YOU

I bless the pathway of promise that you are walking on right now and speak peace. The very pathway itself and the process you are walking is blessed. I pray you will sense God's delight and celebration of you! You are blessed, right now, even while you're still journeying through challenges into victory. I ask for a surge of energy, grace, and miraculous mountain-shifting breakthrough that releases a shift even today.

I bless you, Kingdom hero of faith. I'm blessing all God is already doing, and asking for more of what only He can do in your journey. I prophesy breakthrough and change. I prophesy a release of supernatural joy that strengthens and restores hope in you. You are walking into increasing breakthrough, and I ask God to provide supernatural solutions into every circumstance, in Jesus' name, amen.

DECREE

- Process is not my enemy. Promise is my inheritance.
- I decree that process is not in competition with my promise.
- I can and will thrive right now, in the midst of process.
- God is not withholding His promises from me.
- I am a conqueror who conquers and an overcomer who overcomes.
- I am walking into increasing breakthrough in every area of my life.

Chapter 10

ANNOUNCE A NEW SEASON

The mighty Spirit of the Lord Yahweh is wrapped around me because Yahweh has anointed me, as a messenger to preach good news to the poor. He sent me to heal the wounds of the brokenhearted, to tell captives, "You are free," and to tell prisoners, "Be free from your darkness." I am sent to announce a new season of Yahweh's grace and a time of God's recompense on his enemies, to comfort all who are in sorrow, to strengthen those crushed by despair who mourn in Zion—to give them a beautiful bouquet in the place of ashes, the oil of bliss instead of tears, and the mantle of joyous praise instead of the spirit of heaviness. Because of this, they will be known as Mighty Oaks of Righteousness, planted by Yahweh as a living display of his glory. They will restore ruins from long ago and rebuild what was long devastated. They will renew ruined cities and desolations of past generations.

—ISAIAH 61:1-4 TPT

This passage from Isaiah 61 speaks such hope to those who have walked through long, challenging seasons. One of the keys to shifting a season, is to *"announce a new season,"* and to literally speak over our current circumstances that God is doing something new. There's something about speaking over our season and circumstances that shifts things. Announce a new season.

God encourages us *always*, even in the seasons and days that feel the worst or are the most challenging in terms of what's actually happening. Discouragement is real, and it will "take you out" if not dealt with in the presence of God. The point is though, God *always* breaks off discouragement and evicts heaviness. Heaviness and discouragement, if it has settled in our hearts, leaving no hope for a pathway forward, is a spirit—and it's not the Holy Spirit. This dark spiral of despair is never from God, *never*.

LIGHT BROKE THROUGH

Dwell on thoughts that produce life, and activate faith. We are in charge of what thoughts we dwell on. We can affect our day and season by simply changing what we dwell on, what we focus on, what we think about! Philippians 4:8 tells us, *"Finally, brothers and sisters, whatever is true, whatever is noble, whatever is right, whatever is pure, whatever is lovely, whatever is admirable—if anything is excellent or praiseworthy—think about* [dwell on] *such things."*

Sometimes, it's a choice to make ourselves focus on something positive, and life giving. I have done this in moments when heaviness has tried to take ahold of me on some of the worst days I've walked through. I remember specifically lying in hospital beds in pain with tubes attached to me everywhere, watching worship and sermons that helped my spirit soar. Sometimes though, Ben and I just watched comedy and or cooking shows, a favorite of mine at the time. These simple things helped greatly.

The following simple yet practical things shifted much for me, and I know they'll help you too.

KEYS TO ANNOUNCING A NEW SEASON

1. *Seasons begin, seasons end. Announce a new season.*

I remember some years ago we were going through a *really* hard season that affected our hearts deeply. We had walked through the emotions of disappointments, hurts, betrayals, challenging situations, health struggles, and what seemed like never-ending rolling attacks on every level. As a family this took a toll on our hearts; added to the pain was watching our daughter walk through the hurt of that season too. It just about broke me. The discouragement some days felt overwhelming and never-ending. It seemed that just when things were at the worst, something else happened to make the situation even more devastating. I could go on, but I won't, as anyone who's been alive for more than five minutes has been through something similar. Everyone has walked through *opportunities* to choose forgiveness and let go of offense. The details might be different, but the remedy is the same.

Day after day I felt unable to fully shake the heaviness and deep sadness in me. I spent hours in the prayer room worshipping, soaking, decreeing, crying, and just sitting with God asking Him to hold my heart and keep me from bitterness. I had to forgive a hundred times if not more, until the sting was gone. I remember very clearly the day God said to me, "Jodie, just as seasons begin, seasons end. This season will end."

I can't explain the hope His words gave me. If you are walking through what has felt like an unending season, hear what the Lord is saying to you—this season will end, and new beginnings will spring forth.

Isaiah 61 tells us to *announce a new season!* Yes, speak it forth, prophesy, decree, declare, say it to yourself, and release that something new is springing up. Decree that mourning will pass, and healing will come. Praise will evict heaviness, and joy will replace the tears of despair. Declare a new day. Announce to your own heart; God is doing something new and despair and brokenness are not the end of the story. As we steward our heart well, God will use the preciousness of this season to set you up for promotion, rebuilding what looks ruined, and restoring what seems lost.

I pulled out my words and promises and prophesies and shouted them out! This will pass and the fruit of this season will produce a harvest of oaks, a harvest of righteousness. Increase and multiplication are the fruit of hard seasons given to God as a costly offering. This season will pass. Dance on the places of despair, laugh at the enemy, and announce a new day! Announce a new season till your own heart hears what God is saying.

Our family literally has done this many times. Not long ago we put a bunch of things on the ground that prophetically represented what we were believing for. Then we prayed, had communion, danced, and laughed on top of them. We made it fun—I mean, one look at me and dancing is a comedy act—and it was really powerful. *Immediately* something that had been lost for months was found! Then within hours, we received notification of a significant breakthrough we had only just decreed. This is never about the formula, always about the principle—but as we joyfully announced and decreed a new season, circumstances shifted.

2. *Forgive by choice, not feeling.*

Often, part of announcing a new season is letting "it" go and dealing with the past well. This is serious stuff because I have seen more people taken out of their destiny from unforgiveness and holding on to offense than anything else.

Here's a few practical keys to forgiving and letting go of bitterness and offense:

- If there is any known sin, repent. Then apply grace, reject condemnation, and move on. If you need to say sorry, do it quickly and don't let things fester.

- Apply grace liberally to yourself and to others. When we truly acknowledge that we are not perfect and have hurt others knowingly or unknowingly, it's much easier to apply grace liberally to others. Let's face it, you need grace, so give grace.

- Forgive by choice, not feeling. Forgive by faith, even if you have to say, "Lord, I don't feel like forgiving. I'm not even sure I want to, but I acknowledge that You first forgave me and so I choose to forgive _____. Help me to forgive. Give me *your* grace to forgive, and I trust that the feeling will come later as I do this by obedience and forgive." Sometimes the feeling doesn't come immediately, and usually the hurt doesn't leave all at once. Sometimes it requires daily forgiving over and over, until one day the sting is gone.

- It's possible to forgive without an apology. This is hard, but possible with the oil of grace from Heaven. Forgiving *will* free you. Though apologies are nice, you will not always receive one. Forgiveness is an act of obedience and worship to God, not a response to someone's repentance or lack thereof.

- Offense is insidious. It doesn't matter whether the person did something wrong or not, if you are offended, you are the one who needs to take this to the cross. I'm not saying it's okay what happened. I'm saying your heart health is *your* responsibility, no one else's. If you live life offended all the time, or are carrying offenses from past seasons, it's time to drop the offense and walk free. Don't be mistaken, offense keeps you from promise and walking in the new.

3. *Purposeful praise breaks a spirit of heaviness.*

Sometimes we just have to praise even when we don't feel like it. In fact, that is the exact time to put on some worship music, or show up to church, or jump around silly and speak out His goodness as an act of warfare. Grab Isaiah 61 or Psalm 91 or your favorite Scripture and read it out as a declaration of war! Speak out and sing out God's worth when the heaviness is knocking to move in and take up residence. Dance on despair, I mean it. There's been plenty of times I've had to dance on bad reports and laugh at the enemy's schemes by choice because this breaks the assignment of heaviness and despair. It won't stay, it can't. Praise shifts the atmosphere! When you praise God, you plant seeds of breakthrough.

4. *Joy is not dependent on circumstances.*

"*She* [the Church] *can laugh at the days to come*" (Proverbs 31:25). Joy is a natural response to wonder, breakthrough, and good things; and joy is equally a response to the atmosphere of Heaven infusing us. Supernatural joy comes from His presence: *"in Your presence is fullness of joy"* (Psalm 16:11 NKJV). So do whatever it takes to be in His presence.

Joy is not dependent on circumstances. There is an *"oil of joy,"* which Isaiah 61:3 talks about, that is grace from the glory realm to enter into a supernatural joy that evicts despair and adds peace. This joy makes no sense to the world, but this joy breaks the back of the enemy's schemes and obliterates despair.

"The joy of the Lord is your strength" (Nehemiah 8:10). Take note, it's the joy *of the Lord*—it's not dependent on *your* joy, current feelings, or circumstances. It comes from God. Leaning into supernatural joy shifts the atmosphere and your season. We can decree joy over our new season, regardless of how we feel, because it is our inheritance. The joy of the Lord is *your* strength and inheritance. That is your promise, speak it out and laugh it out over your season.

AN EARTHQUAKE IN MY PRAYER ROOM

During this hard season, I would spend hours in our prayer room. I would often be awake in the pre-dawn hours and sit and watch the sunrise. It did my soul good and stirred hope every time. I listened over and over and over to the song from Bethel Music, "It is Well" by Kristene Dimarco. Then I'd listen to it over again! You get the picture. I needed to lean in and decree, "It is well, it is well with my soul." I encourage you to listen to it, some of the words are:

> *This mountain that's in front of me*
> *Will be thrown into the midst of the sea.*
> *And through it all, through it all*
> *My eyes are on You*
> *And through it all, through it all*

171

It is well
So let go my soul and trust in Him
The waves and wind still know His name
So let go my soul and trust in Him
The waves and wind still know His name
And it is well with my soul
It is well with my soul
And through it all, through it all
My eyes are on You
And it is well with me

I would literally listen to this song every time my insides felt crushed and wounded. It became the soundtrack and declaration of my season.

One day in the middle of that season, I was home alone while Ben and Keely were in India on another mission trip. I remember being downstairs in the kitchen of our split-level home. The prayer room was at the very top corner of the home and looked out over the suburb, so it was perfect for praying over the region. It was a beautiful place to pray as the sun came up. But that day I couldn't stop thinking of all that was going on and wondering if I would ever feel myself again, would it ever not hurt? Would the shaking and storm ever stop?

Suddenly, I felt an urgent compelling to go to the prayer room and listen to that song and decree "It is well!" I turned up the volume loud and started shouting and marching in my prayer room, as I spoke out over myself, my family, church, and region. I remember a militancy came on me as I yelled out, "IT IS WELL, THE WAVES AND WIND STILL KNOW HIS NAME, THIS MOUNTAIN THAT'S IN FRONT OF ME

WILL BE THROWN INTO THE SEA. IT IS WELL WITH MY SOUL!"

Literally within 60 seconds of being in the prayer room and shouting and praying, suddenly, the ground began to shake! Like *really* shake. Our house was swaying and shaking violently back and forth. I was suddenly aware an earthquake was happening, which was very rare on the Sunshine Coast of Australia. I went to the doorway of the prayer room and stood shouting, "IT IS WELL" with music blasting throughout our house, "IT IS WELL, IT IS WELL!"

Aside from it being a little disconcerting, it was actually very comedic with the house shaking, music blaring, and me yelling at the top of my lungs, "IT IS WELL, IT IS WELL"! When the shaking stopped, such a weighty presence of God fell on me. I knew God was reminding me that the shaking would not shake me—that it was well with my soul.

New Zealand Earthquake

I was immediately reminded of ministering in Christchurch, New Zealand in 2012 when suddenly, what I can only best describe as a "bubble of light and peace" dropped on me as I was prophesying life over Christchurch. This city had suffered much devastation after a huge earthquake only six months before. Just walking around, we could feel that the atmosphere carried a heavy, tangible sense of despair and fear. It was thick and consuming. People were scared and lacking hope to rebuild their lives.

I must also say, the unity and prayers of the church there really turned the tide as hope arose in the months to come! When this "bubble" dropped on me though, a heightened sense of God's glory and presence was released, and I started decreeing passionately, "Life, life, life over Christchurch. Life, life, life to the city of Christchurch." I was completely engulfed in this prophetic bubble and somehow unaware of anything else until "it" lifted and I finished.

When I finished prophesying, I noticed Keely looked a little shocked, and later Ben said, "How crazy was that earthquake?"

"What earthquake?" I asked. Apparently, there had been an earthquake that shook the entire church and caused some concern. I had been prophesying LIFE the entire way through the earthquake, completely oblivious to the shaking! I wasn't trying to just carry on bravely in the midst of the shaking, I was in such a *bubble* of peace and presence prophesying life that the only thing I was aware of was what God was saying. Later I heard God whisper to me, "Though the earth may shake, you will not be shaken."

God is with His people; even as shaking happens, we can say, "It is well with our soul." And as "things" shake, prophesy LIFE and life abundant! God was making it clear in two different earthquakes that our voice, our decrees, and our partnering with the King and prophesying life is imperative.

Though the earth may shake, you can know, "It is well with my soul, I will not be shaken." The shaking is not your identity. The seal of the King marks you, and your identity is found in the security of who you are in the Lord. Something that made me proud as a mum, is that Keely, who was only 12 at the time, continued playing the keyboard during the earthquake. Despite having eyes wide open with a look of "What the heck is going on?" she didn't miss a beat.

So as I stood in my prayer room in another earthquake that day shouting, "IT IS WELL!" I heard the echo of my faithful friend and King speaking deeply to my soul:, "Jodie, all will be well, the winds and rain still know My name, you can trust Me to remove this mountain to the sea, because of who I am. The shaking will cease, the season will pass, and even while it shakes, it is well with you My child, for the shaking cannot touch you." I hear Him whispering the same to you.

As God had said it would, the season shifted, and new beginnings seemed everywhere. That season of discouragement did indeed end.

Interestingly, it was not long after this hard season that the Pineapple Revival broke out. I thank God for all He taught me, and us, in the season of shaking. Thank God He healed the brokenness and despair and strengthened us with His joy. Thank God we kept going.

You too, friend, keep going. The season *will* change. Announce a new season. Decree a new day. Speak to the storm and say, "Be still." Proclaim new beginnings and decree, "It is well with my soul and my season."

THE KING'S DECREE FOR YOU

"My Holy Spirit is upon you. I have anointed you as My messenger. I have anointed you to announce a new season. I am giving you beauty for ashes and a spirit of praise for a spirit of heaviness. My child, announce a new season, for you are anointed."

—THE KING

MY PRAYER FOR YOU

I announce a new season of joy, harvest, and fulfilled promise to you. The days of heaviness and loss are over and the days of heart-stirring joy are here. I ask the Lord to open doors that lead to establishing destiny and restoring what the enemy tried to destroy. I speak life in the midst of the storm, healing where you need it, and rebuilding where the enemy tried to tear you down. I pray that you will say and mean it, "IT IS WELL WITH MY SOUL." I decree over you, "It is well with your soul." I'm blessing your heart to thrive in this season. The season has changed, my friend, and I decree miracles, salvations, healing, provision, solutions, restoration, and devil-stomping victories that cause you to laugh at the days to come. In Jesus' name, amen.

DECREE

- I decree I will not be shaken. I can laugh at the days to come.
- I decree the season has shifted; winter has passed and spring has come.
- I decree it is well!
- I prophesy over my season:
    it is well with my soul,
    it is well with my season,
    it is well with my circumstances,
    it is well with my family,
    it is well with my finances,
    it is well with my nation.

- It is well with my heart.
- It is well with my soul.

Chapter 11

THE ZERUBBABEL MANDATE

"This is the word of the Lord to Zerubbabel: 'Not by might nor by power, but by my Spirit,' says the Lord Almighty. What are you, mighty mountain? Before Zerubbabel you will become level ground. Then he will bring out the capstone to shouts of 'God bless it! God bless it!'"
—ZECHARIAH 4:6-7

AWAKENED BY AN ANGEL

Eleven years ago, Ben and I were awakened in the night by a 10-foot angel standing on the end of our bed. Yes, we screamed! What was one of the greatest miracles of this encounter was that our 10-year-old daughter, Keely, didn't wake up hearing both her parents screaming at the top of their lungs! I had encounters before, but *nothing* like this! I first saw the angel while I was asleep, opened my eyes, and he was still there standing on our bed, staring at us. The angel was brighter than light, wore a golden sash, and we knew he was there to wake us up and deliver a message from God. I remember the eyes, they glared with intensity of purpose.

We often share this encounter with others because it literally changed our lives and launched Pour It Out Ministries. Whenever we talk about it, there is a transferable fear of the Lord and a release of miracles. So be expectant.

I immediately knew the angel was on a mission from the throne room of Heaven, as the weighty glory he emanated was intense. It felt like electricity coursing through me and the fear of the Lord was tangible in every fiber of my being. I was immediately aware that holiness matters, purity matters, character matters, and hearing, "Well done good and faithful servant," was my life purpose. This was an encounter from the Lord that would mark our lives forever.

There was such a tangible presence of God that all I did was scream and hit Ben over and over, yelling, "THERE'S AN ANGEL! THERE'S AN ANGEL!" Ben woke up screaming too, and later said he felt electricity literally rolling up and down his body. I knew this was God answering our prayers as we'd been asking God for more and for ministry direction. The whole encounter carried a weight of fire and holiness that was terrifying in a holy and wondrous way. The intensity of God's weighty glory and His manifest presence was thick and undeniably holy.

THE FEAR OF THE LORD

When the angel left, a "blanket" of the holy fear of the Lord fell over the room. This manifestation of the fear of the Lord was so consuming that I barely spoke for months as every part of my heart was being weighed and measured. That level of awareness of God's realness and holiness was precious. So much so that when I would start to speak, I'd find myself unable to as there was such a purifying of my heart attitudes, hidden motives, or agendas. I found myself constantly asking myself, *Does this honor the Lord? Am I speaking in love? Do I really mean that?* Every part of our life and heart was laid bare before the Lord as He released refining fire.

God birthed Pour It Out Ministries from this encounter as He showed us Zechariah 4 and revealed He was calling us to "pour out the oil of His presence and power" in the nations. This was a commissioning encounter with an angel of awakening. And nothing has been the same since! It marked us with new levels of fire, fear of the Lord, and awakening. Leading up to this night we had been called into a five-month extended time of prayer and pressing in. We would pray and worship between four to eight hours a day as we were desperate for God to move. We were desperate for more of God. There was a holy frustration in us that there must be more, and we must have it—and so we pressed in.

We had seen and done so much at this point. We had been staff pastors in a large church, senior pastors of a smaller church, pioneered cafe churches, youth movements, planted several churches, been in leadership roles of many different types of churches, served, given, and wholeheartedly pursued the call of God on our lives... but this encounter still changed everything! A healthy dose of the fear of the Lord reminded us what mattered most. There was a hunger imparted that was insatiable, contagious, and uncontained.

So the words of Zechariah 4, *"Not by might nor by power, but by my Spirit says the Lord Almighty"* deeply spoke to our hearts. As did, *"Do not despise the day of small beginnings"* and *"What are you, mighty mountain? Before Zerubbabel you will become level ground."* These words were forged into my spirit.

As we stepped out into a new season of revival ministry, the miracles and fire were noticeably different. Supernatural signs, wonders, and miracles flowed in ways they hadn't before. Breakthrough was being imparted in significant ways with souls, healings, and life-changing encounters taking place with power we hadn't seen before.

STILL BATTLING

I was still battling with health challenges despite previous times of significant healing. There had been different complications and effects of long-term medicine and illness that took a toll on my body and required constant contending for full healing. Then my health took a sharp turn for the worse. I remember times of ministering and the anointing coming and I would feel well, and then I'd come away from the meeting barely able to stand because of the pain. We knew it wasn't God, we knew God was good, and we knew we were not giving up contending for what God had begun.

Our finances were completely depleted as bills mounted and Ben was increasingly unable to leave the house due to my worsening health. Truly Ben was and is incredible. There are victories I'm walking in today that I wouldn't be in if it weren't for his faith and determination to not give up decreeing.

As you know now, it wasn't the first time I'd faced severe health obstacles. It wasn't the first time I'd faced giants I thought we had slaughtered in a past season. You may be facing battles with giants that seem to have raised their head again too. I am praying complete breakthrough for you.

To put some context in the situation, I was stuck in the bathroom 20-40 times a day, unable to eat properly, extremely weak, and without energy to do much at all except try to look after Keely and be the best mum I could. Actually, Keely and I built a very special bond during these years, and it has often been her prayers that touched my heart so deeply. I will never forget one day she was praying and massaging my back to help me feel better, gold appeared right on the sore spot! I know right! Amazing. As she rubbed my back, right where the gold appeared, the soreness in my back *completely* left! God is so cool.

I had great doctors and good advice and treatment, but it just wasn't working and complications often made things worse. At this point, I lived 24/7 with constant need for the bathroom or threat thereof—sorry to talk about bathrooms so much, it's just that was the realness of my situation that effected everything! But by the grace of God, I managed to minister, travel, homeschool, and do life—did I say with *lots* of grace?! Actually, it was revival fire and God's manifest presence that kept me going.

One day when Ben was away ministering in the United States, I went to my specialist as I was in pain. He told me to *immediately* go to the hospital emergency room, as he held grave concerns. I first went home to take Keely to my good friend's house to look after her, and I also wanted to take a moment at home to pray before putting myself in that environment. I knew enough to know I needed the Word of the Lord to hold on to, and to turn down the volume of every other voice but God's. I needed to call out to the God of the breakthrough and take a moment to still my heart and lean into the atmosphere of Heaven.

SUDDENLY, ZERUBBABEL

I was sitting on the lounge chair praying in my living room, the TV was on and I could faintly hear a news channel in the background. I prayed and waited to hear from God. I could hear the TV presenter reading the news as I prayed, and then *suddenly* a static-type sound cut across the news, and a voice spoke very loudly from the TV. The voice said, "ZERUBBABEL." My spirit leapt. Then just as suddenly, the TV presenter continued reading the news! I was immediately aware that God just spoke to me through my TV!

Yes, I could hardly believe it myself. God spoke to me and prophesied from the very chapter that He commissioned us from, when an angel stood on our bed. I knew it was wild, yet God just interrupted the TV somehow and spoke the word of the Lord to me, "ZERUBBABEL!"

Well I knew right away what God was saying. If God was calling out to me "Zerubbabel," then He was telling me to get up and decree, "Oh mighty mountain who are you, you are nothing before the hand of Zerubbabel!" God was commanding me to decree. To speak. To not be overwhelmed by the mountain, but to speak to the mountain. To get up on my feet and command the mountain that thinks it's mighty that it is indeed nothing, and that at my voice, at my decree it will indeed be melted like wax and become nothing but level ground.

This obstacle would become a level pathway to the promises of God on my life. The mountain of sickness and pain and everything that had risen to threaten the call of God on my life would be broken. Using *my* voice and at *my* decree, I knew God was saying, "Speak to the mountain Jodie." I decreed, "Meet the God of the breakthrough. Meet the God of all things are possible. Meet the

God who says, 'Not by might nor by power but by My Spirit.' I release His Spirit right now. I release His power. I release the Spirit of God bringing breakthrough where there seems to be no way!"

I prayed for quite a while and decreed the Word of the Lord from Zechariah 4 spoken to Zerubbabel. Nothing will stand in the way of Zerubbabel. What God has begun He will complete, and small beginnings do not prophesy delay, they prophesy completion. So I commanded every assignment of the enemy to bow before the hand of the Lord.

At Zerubbabel's Hand

God was making a profound point. Zerubbabel was a person just like us. He was an official working to restore the temple of God, but He was just a man with a call and a job who faced an obstacle that prevented him from moving forward. God was reminding me that He uses our voice, our hands, and our faith to level mountains. He was reminding me that my voice is powerful and my faith partnered with God's truth is a mighty force of change that speaks to the impossible and sees breakthrough come.

God was saying—open your mouth, speak Zerubbabel, get up and prophesy Zerubbabel, tell this mountain to meet the God who decimates the plans of the enemy. Tell this mountain to meet the God who smashes mountains that arrogantly prophesy obstruction of God's promises in your life. God was reminding me—don't be impressed by the mountain, it's not actually mighty, it's just dirt in the way of God's plans that will be flattened as you decree and prophesy to the mountain.

There is something powerful about standing in the face of fear, holding on to truth and courageously speaking out the Word of the Lord. God is inviting us to stop speaking *about* the mountain and speak *to* the mountain! We have the authority of the King to speak miracles, signs, and wonders. There are moments in all of our lives when mountains stand in the way, but we have been given authority, by the name of the King, to decree the Word of the Lord—just like Zerubbabel was. Not only have we been given authority to decree to the mountains, God is urging us and compelling us, "Zerubbabel, open your mouth, stretch out your hand."

> *"This is the word of the Lord to Zerubbabel: 'Not by might nor by power, but by My Spirit,' says the Lord of hosts"* (Zechariah 4:6 NKJV).

Zerubbabels are arising who have a mandate to speak to obstacles and decree them to be scattered before the people of God and release mountain-leveling faith. Their voices will birth the beginnings of miracles that will astound and their hands will also see the completion of what God begins. The enemy may rise up to interrupt, disrupt, and try and undo what God has begun, but the Zerubbabel anointing will not let go of what God has said until it is completed with great shouts of *"Grace, grace to it!"* (Zechariah 4:7 NKJV). Grace. Grace over the mountains in your life—before *you* they shall become level ground.

Those who decree *"by My Spirit"* will pour out the oil of His presence and power with great boldness. They know God is the chain breaker and mountain leveler. Jesus talks about mountains in the way and tells us in Matthew 17:20:

> *Truly I tell you, if you have faith as small as a mustard seed, you can say to this mountain, "Move from here to there," and it will move. Nothing will be impossible for you.*

I release this mountain-moving faith to you. I speak this Zerubbabel mandate to you—by My Spirit level mountains. No mountain in the way of what God has spoken to you is permitted to prophesy to you.

Arise Zerubbabel! Zerubbabels are those who bring break-through, regardless of the mountains in the way. Zerubbabels are just regular people who grab hold of the authority given as sons and daughters of the King. When we grab hold of this truth, we too, just like Zerubbabel, will achieve great exploits for God, even in the midst of great resistance.

Arise woman or man of God. Arise, mighty warrior. This mountain looks mighty, but it is a liar. It is not what the Lord is speaking. And the God of mountain-moving faith is speaking to Zerubbabels all across the nations even now and is charging *your* voice, *your* anointing, and *your* hand to complete every assignment that He has placed on your life. He is anointing your voice to stand, speak, arise, and prophesy: "Oh mighty mountain, who are you? You will be nothing but level ground."

Nothing can stand in the way of what God has spoken. What God has started He will complete, and so we command this mountain to move and be level ground. I speak breakthrough and grace to complete every last word God has spoken over your life. The things that have declared, "You will not pass," we instead declare they will become the very pathway that your feet will walk on into breakthrough.

THE KING'S DECREE FOR YOU

"It is not by your might or by your power—but it is by My Spirit. You have My Spirit within you, My child. Speak, 'Grace, grace' over every circumstance. You have authority to tell every mountain to be level ground. Let's together watch those mighty mountains become level plains as you open your mouth."

—THE KING

MY PRAYER FOR YOU

I prophesy and release resurrection life over you, mighty warrior. You are a mountain-leveler who sees breakthrough at your hand and decree. You pour out His love, power, and presence in the nations as you bless small beginnings because you know they prophesy great completions. Your voice is anointed to tell the works of the enemy to make way, as God is always finding a way forward and making obstacles and mountains level ground. You speak and mountains move. I decree nothing will stand in the way of what God has called you to. I call in revival fire to mark you, refuel you, embolden and empower you. In Jesus' name, amen.

DECREE

- ~ I decree mountains of impossibility become level ground before me.
- ~ It is not by might or by power but by His Spirit.

- I do not partner with fear or pressure, I partner with the decree of the King who lifts every load so I can walk in freedom!

- I carry the fire of God. I am a fire carrier, a fire releaser, and a fire catalyst. People encounter God around me.

Chapter 12

JUSTICE AND MERCY ENCOUNTER

God is not unjust; he will not forget your work
and the love you have shown him as you have
helped his people and continue to help them.
—HEBREWS 6:10

Some of the best advice I ever heard, but didn't want to hear the day it was said to me was, "Even if 'they' do everything wrong, you are still called to do everything right."

It hit home, I knew it was truth—but goodness that was hard to hear and even harder to do. I was in my 20s and had been pioneering a ministry project; and as life goes sometimes, things changed and I was caught up in the mess of people stuff. I had been hurt and was struggling with the injustice of being wrongly accused. I was genuinely trying hard to push off offense but I really felt betrayed and wronged. That advice hit me though as if God Himself was sitting across the cafe table speaking them to me.

I prayed. I forgave. I asked for help to let it go, but my heart still felt wronged. The inner justice meter in me was demanding things be set straight; I hated that untruth had been spoken of me. The injustice of the situation was causing me heartache. You may be able to relate.

As I wrestled with letting it go in my heart, dealing with the pain of being misunderstood, and feeling like my efforts for God had been wasted and ruined, I suddenly heard a Bible reference clearly in my spirit, *"Hebrews 6:10."* It was a clear, still-small-voice word. I had no idea what this verse was at the time, so as you can imagine, I quickly looked it up:

> *God is not unjust; he will not forget your work and the love you have shown him as you have helped his people and continue to help them* (Hebrews 6:10).

Wow. I cried. I knew God was speaking directly to my situation. I knew He was sharing a deep truth I needed to hear that would sustain me through not just this circumstance, but many situations to come.

Even if people and situations are unjust, God is not, and I needed to hear that. I needed to get that deep down. Our work is ultimately for God, not people; and pleasing the heart of God is the ultimate prize. God takes it personally when we love people and help them, wow. God considers our efforts as loving Him, and He will not forget, even if people do.

God also wanted me to hear through His Word, to not quit serving Him, and continue in my call even when things happen, because things happen. He basically was saying, "Don't let stuff with people, and the inevitable hurts, criticisms, injustices, and the 'real moments' of ministry life be a roadblock to loving Me and following your call. Remember, it's *Me* you're working for, and I never forget anything you sacrifice and give to Me."

Lots of tears later, I felt the tenderness of God and I knew God was putting a foundational truth in my heart that if I really took this on, it would prevent me from being derailed in my life purpose by offense and people stuff. Oh, how many times I've leaned into that verse since, and it really has kept me going through thick and thin. It's literally been a life-saving verse. Injustice happens; but God is *not* unjust. And we can trust Him even when things happen that are hard to rise above. What's more, the goal is to not just "get through," but to come through with a soft heart, not with a chip on our shoulder.

Sometimes it's like we repeat the lesson a few times so the potency of the truth is embedded in the core of our being, instead of it just being mental ascent. This was one of those hard truths to learn but a destiny-saving key: even if "they" do everything wrong, we are still called to do everything right. Stewarding my heart meant taking ownership of my stuff and my responses, which isn't always easy, but it defines those who finish their race.

I have fought the good fight, I have finished the race, I have kept the faith (2 Timothy 4:7).

Our heart responses are ours alone to steward. This hit home with great weight in that moment. I knew I could only do that with God's help. My heart wanted to tell a bunch of people off and start a mutiny! "Jesus, help my heart," became my prayer. You know, funny things happen with prayers like that. Jesus actually helps! And I discovered I had a bunch of areas to mature in as well and needed to allow God to grow my character and mold my heart. This truth was laid as a foundation in my heart. And wow, I'm thankful God taught me this truth, because I needed it in the years that followed.

But—God Delivers

Ben and I had been hungering after the "more" of God for a long time. Our entire married life has really been marked by a passionate pursuit of God's heart. Yes there have been ups, downs, and plenty of moments needing grace, but we have always been hungry for more.

But stuff happens in life, and again we found ourselves hurt and betrayed. Our dear friend Larry Taylor often says, "Why does God use imperfect people? Because they're the only kind He's got!" If I want God to use me, I need to be okay with Him using others because we are all imperfect. If we are going to serve God, we had better get past people needing to be perfect in order to honor them. But as for me, I was still learning this on a deeper level.

A resolve was being formulated in me to not be moved by the critics and attackers—but only be moved by the voice of God. This is a huge deal for all believers; as attacks come, hard seasons, persecution, and injustices happen along the journey—the question really is, will these challenges move me off my course?

God is restoring the plumb line of purity and righteousness in the body and I think we can sense that. There is a call from Heaven to consecration and purifying our hearts. This is actually because of His mercy. God is pouring out greater glory, and without greater fear of the Lord, we will be unable to steward well the weightiness of what is about to come. In fact, without greater fear of the Lord, the coming glory will break us, instead of make us. The prayer to "Create in me a clean heart," is actually His grace and His goodness.

As we walked through another situation where there was a sense of betrayal, slander, and loss, I could feel even in the midst of it that God was purifying my heart. Sadly, the situation was causing ministry bookings to cancel, and so it made us wonder if our ministry could survive the hit. The attack and false judgments deeply hurt. Our ministry future seemed unsure, our finances had taken a huge hit, and our hearts were really bleeding and hurting.

This time of turmoil reminds me of a sermon I had heard years ago, "When you're cut, what do you bleed? Do you bleed bitterness, or do you bleed worship?" Ben and I felt the tenderness of God drawing us into the safety of His heart. We spent a lot of time shutting off the chatter and noise and leaning into worship. It saved us then; it saves us now.

I think what is often not talked about enough in times of attack, injustice, or persecution is that *"Our struggle is not against flesh and blood, but against the rulers, against the authorities, against the powers of this dark world and against the spiritual forces of evil in the heavenly realms"* (Ephesians 6:12). There is a very real spirit realm that is unleashed against the saints with intent to harm, and requires prayer and decreeing truth to break its effects. This spirit tries to muzzle our voice, paralyze our progress, and get us "stuck" in offense to derail our call. *However,* this spirit is subject to Jesus! Say with me, "The name of Jesus is higher!"

Determining to decree truth and silence the voice of the accuser in times like this will save you. Worship needs to be louder than the chatter. Stay remembering that God is not unjust even when injustice is happening, and that He will not forget you as you walk through to the other side. Decree, "No weapon formed against me will prosper" (Isaiah 54:17), hide your heart in worship, and listen for what God is saying about you. Stay in honor, seek God's face, and put your trust in Him. Of course, do whatever God shows you to do; but my encouragement is, take time to get your heart right before you *respond*, otherwise you will *react* rather than *respond*.

It's important to point out that God is always bigger than what the enemy is doing, and what we focus on is magnified. Focusing on and decreeing His goodness is good practice—always. Focus on God, not the enemy.

As I retell this time in our lives, I am very aware that although none of this was fun and none of it was God's heart, it wasn't so much about the details of this situation as it was the demonic assault to halt our call and destroy our destiny and trust in God. We all walk through similar situations and the enemy's intention is *always* the same—to cause us to become so bitter or broken that we give up and walk away. The accuser wants our voice silenced. But God wants our voice amplified. Stewarding our hearts even when faced with injustice, brings promotion and increase into your life.

Two Bright Lights

I couldn't stop crying. Literally, I just couldn't stop crying. I'm not one to fall apart easily. I'm usually strong and my most common response to challenges is to put on my armor and fight, but I felt really heartbroken. Ben had to scoop me up off the floor and hold me while I cried and cried and cried—and couldn't stop. That made me feel worse though, as despite his kindness, I felt a failure because I just couldn't get on top of it. The spiritual side of the attack seemed overwhelming at the time. Thoughts kept coming at me, "Quit and never pursue ministry again, it's not worth it." I was determined to not quit, but I felt so weak, and I needed help.

I knew this battle was spiritual, and I knew it was a fork-in-the-road moment. I also knew I needed my King Jesus to help. We prayed and we decreed, but for me the prayers were mostly just broken simple words and tears. I finally fell asleep sobbing.

At some point in the night I woke up and saw two bright lights shining on both sides of our bed. Each light had a vague form of a person standing tall, but shining light enough to make them just visible. I understood immediately they were angelic, but I was so exhausted and broken that I didn't pay a lot of attention except that it felt *very* peaceful. Miraculously, I immediately went back to sleep.

When I woke up in the morning, the first thing I noticed was the consuming "sting" was gone. I was still hurting, I still felt betrayed—but the sting in my heart was completely gone. And then I realized that I wasn't crying. I had finally stopped crying.

Later that day when I was quiet and able to think and pray, I knew something supernatural had taken place and God did something precious.

I prayed and simply asked, "God, what were those angels I saw last night?"

Immediately I clearly heard, "Justice and Mercy."

I thought about it and said, "Justice I understand God because clearly I want justice poured out, but why was Mercy here?"

Again I clearly heard in response, "Because I'm pouring out Justice, you need Mercy too.'

Woah. That hit me like a ton of bricks as the fear of the Lord infused my heart. It suddenly dawned on me with deeper revelation that I needed mercy too! Even when divine justice is administered, we all need God's mercy. The truth of this penetrated deep.

How thankful I was that God removed the sting and healed my soul. In the weeks, months, and even in the years later, we've watched as God brought justice. God showed us when to speak, and mostly when not to. Learning a deeper revelation of the power of honor has been a game changer. I've found ever since, that unless my heart is in honor, I have no business speaking into something.

We knew God was saying, "Stay in honor, trust in Me. I am not unjust and I will not forget all you do for Me." He hasn't, He *never* has. In fact, there's been many times since when favor has opened doors that we couldn't; and we have known…this is from our King who is *not* unjust and remembers our private battles and victories.

I didn't walk the journey perfectly, far from it. But I'm forever grateful for that night Justice and Mercy stood at the end of my bed, healing my heart, and expanding my understanding of God's character and kindness. God also put deep resolve in my heart— the critics do not open doors for me, only God does. God is the door opener! Truly God is the God who opens doors no one can close (Isaiah 22:22).

A depth of fear of the Lord was released when Justice and Mercy stood in our bedroom. I write this with tears and with compassion—we all need grace and we all need mercy, even our enemies. A moment of authenticity does our hearts good. Jesus said, pray for your enemies and *"bless those who curse you"* (Matthew 5:44 NKJV). The thing is, everyone needs mercy, our enemies, and ourselves included.

Praying blessing over our enemies frees us. This isn't easy, in fact it's really hard. I have learned to do this by faith and trust God for the feelings later, sometimes much later. I remember when

God said to me, "Don't hold people captive to the worst day of their worst season. Set the captive free from your own heart, Jodie." Wow, and tears. This is the real stuff. This is the stuff that can't be done without supernatural grace for forgiveness.

I realized that I had kept people captive in my own heart, and I needed to set them free. It didn't make it okay, but it certainly set my heart free. I understand you may have walked through horrendous, grievous things. I also know God's grace and healing for us is bigger than what we have walked through. That's my prayer for you, your heart set free.

> *The Spirit of the Lord is upon me, for he has anointed me to bring Good News to the poor. He has sent me to proclaim that captives will be released, that the blind will see, that the oppressed will be set free* (Luke 4:18 NLT).

Sometimes setting the captives free starts with us. Set the captives free from your own heart, as it's time these chains that keep us captive are broken in Jesus' name. It was for freedom Jesus came, and I decree freedom to your heart (read Galatians 5:1). I pray God's tenderness to you, and great grace, mighty one.

> *It is for freedom that Christ has set us free...* (Galatians 5:1).

ANGER—AN UNWANTED SIDE EFFECT

Often when dealing with injustice and well, "stuff," I would find myself getting angry. When I become angry in one area of my life, it seems to spill into every other area of my life, and basically I become an angry person. I think that's the same for most people. This was happening in that season. I was just angry about almost everything. Even things that were good were being tainted in my heart and I was in need of an "oil change."

Have you ever had a conversation in your head where you're speaking to situations and getting more and more worked up in your thoughts? Come on, I'm sure this isn't just me. Well, I was in the middle of one of those nighttime conversations in my head when I heard the Holy Spirit clearly say, "Psalm 37:8." I had no idea what that Bible verse said so I looked it up:

> *Stop being angry! Turn from your rage! Do not lose your temper—it only leads to harm* (Psalm 37:8 NLT).

Oh goodness! God definitely answered me! I didn't feel told off at all; rather, I felt the kindness of God urging me to realign my heart. Well, as you can imagine, I had an honest, raw moment right then and there with God as I gave Him my anger, and asked again for Him to, *"Create in me a clean heart"* (Psalm 51:10 NLT). This heart journey with God requires vulnerability.

BLESSED ARE YOU WHEN YOU ARE PERSECUTED

This seems like a strange thing to say, but I've come to realize, in a fear-of-the-Lord kind of way, the preciousness of going through hard seasons and coming out the other side with the Lord. Please don't think I'm aligning my small sufferings with those who are martyred and attacked for the gospel, this is precious in the sight of the Lord. I am, however, aligning all of our sufferings in any shape or form, as a place of intimate connection to God. When we go through something because the enemy has come against us, Jesus says we are blessed.

Blessed are those who are persecuted for righteousness' sake, for theirs is the kingdom of heaven (Matthew 5:10 NKJV).

I have since walked though many other challenging times and victorious wins with Jesus. And in the quiet moments with God, I've found myself saying this verse and thanking God for the hard places we've walked through together, and what I've learned and grown in. This has built a strength that I know has enabled me to stand in other situations. Without what I learned "back then," I know I could not have stood now. I know without what I gained in "the valley," I could not have stewarded what God was pouring out on the mountain.

"Blessed are those who are persecuted"—I say it with the fear of the Lord on my lips and a trembling in my soul. I don't want to ever walk through those things again, but I equally hold precious what the Lord tenderly and ever so kindly showed me in those times.

If you've been through a season where attack seems like it's coming from every side and your heart is hurting, I speak great blessing over you. The Kingdom of Heaven is yours! What does that really mean? It means the very atmosphere of the throne room, the glory of our future home, is being given to you right now in the middle of what you are going through. God is releasing His justice to move on your behalf. You are loved and cherished and celebrated in Heaven right now. Heaven is cheering you on. This too shall pass, and you will arise stronger and wiser and carrying something of Heaven that you hadn't experienced before.

Please hear my heart—God doesn't send harm your way to grow you. He is not the author of persecution or destructive seasons. God is well able to show you fresh revelation and love through

His kindness and goodness, and He does. God does forge strength in the fire though. He is close to the brokenhearted in a unique way and does not leave you in times of distress or attack. He is championing you in a way that you will remember for the rest of your days. It's in these moments when the world seems against you, that we truly discover, "If my God is for me, who can be against me?" (See Romans 8:31.)

As for me, I am eternally grateful for the tender care and justice of the Lord that I found on my worst days. I am blessed not because of "persecution" but because I found the roaring heart of my King standing with me, and for me. And when I couldn't fight anymore, I found God fiercely fighting for me. I'm equally thankful that God showed me in my own heart journey that I too need mercy and grace. It makes it a whole lot easier to forgive others, when we are confronted with the imperfections, sin and messy places in our hearts. Yes I desire justice, and yes I need mercy. Lord, thank You for Your mercy and grace in my own life. We all need forgiveness. We all need mercy.

Because of the nature of what I am talking about in this chapter, I want to add that God is emphasizing justice in this season. He is bringing justice to many current issues and areas that need the roar of Heaven to bring alignment to righteousness. God is raising up many "justice warriors" and those who will contend in prayer and action for justice. Justice on a broad scale is about wrongs being addressed and victims receiving redemption. Justice is as much from the throne room as mercy and grace are, and I believe that God's heart for those harmed by unrighteousness will be seen in a fresh and plumb-line-establishing way in this season.

"God is not unjust" (Hebrews 6:10). I don't presume for a moment to align my "momentary hurts" with those who have

walked through horrific things. I do know though, the stories may be different, but our God is the same, and He is not unjust.

It's not what comes against us, it's how we respond and rise above it that counts. Those who run to God will be the voices of hope, purity and justice that influence their generation.

THE KING'S DECREE FOR YOU

"My child, I am not unjust. I have seen every yes in your heart. I have seen your love for Me and every good thing you have done. You can rest in this. My voice and My opinion matter most. I love you with an unconditional love. Let My love fill every broken part of your heart."

—THE KING

MY PRAYER FOR YOU

I speak blessing to your heart right now. I pronounce Justice and Mercy are sent to you from the throne room and God is fiercely protecting your heart and call. I bless you with comfort, healing, and peace from the Holy Spirit poured out over you today. I call in Justice where you've been robbed, and thank You, God, for pouring out abundant kindness and goodness on my friend. I pray for God's tender presence to be close to you right now and that He will lead you into favor that will bless every part of your life. I prophesy new authority on you to be a justice warrior as you pray, and prophesy that your decrees are affecting nations and your own community. I bless you with an anointing to set the captives free. God's hand is upon you. I pray an impenetrable shield of grace around you and a harvest bursting open from seeds faithfully sown.

DECREE

- I rise above whatever comes against me.
- My heart is stilled in the presence of God. I am blessed today, and tomorrow. My future is blessed.
- I am not alone—for God is with me.
- As I love others and serve the Lord, I give all I am and all I do as an offering to God.

Chapter 13

FOR MY MUM— HEAVEN'S REALITY

Where, O death, is your sting?
—1 CORINTHIANS 15:55

I'm so thankful I know I will see my mum again. The day she went to Heaven is one of the most glorious and heart-wrenching days of my life. God gave me a gift that day that changed how I view death. More to the point, it changed how I view life.

During their time in India as missionaries, my parents had seen all kinds of miracles, healings, and even the dead raised to life. Mum had fought cancer before and came through with a clean bill of health. When she was suddenly diagnosed with cancer a second time, both my parents and Ben and I had full faith and complete expectation she would again be healed.

We rushed to make plans and get Mum back to Australia for medical treatment and to be with family as we prayed and believed, and spent time just loving her through the battle. As soon as she got off the flight, though, one look at her in a wheelchair, something I'd never seen before, told me she was in a bad way. Again though, her faith and our faith was expectant. We all had seen many miracles. Being brutally honest, we had all seen healings and miracles every time we ministered, which I'm only mentioning because I know it will encourage some that we all face situations that are seemingly contradictory and don't always make sense. I think we've all been there, when what we are experiencing isn't what we prayed for, or believed for, and we don't understand.

PRAYING FOR OTHERS

In times like this, people need love, they need prayer, they need our faith to believe and stand with them. Sadly, some too often start judging or attacking the wounded while they are fighting the battle of—and for—their lives. Can we agree to love, support, and add our faith to their battle, not our criticisms or unsolicited advice. It truly grieves me when I see those in battles being beaten up by the body. I think we can grow at this. I think we can do better. I think we will see more miracles across the body as we continue to grow in standing together and contending in this way.

Coming to terms with some things not making sense is a big deal in the body of Christ. Sometimes there isn't a reason we can understand this side of eternity other than things happen we just don't *get*. Our role is to love, contend, and stand with each other in the realness of life. If we are honest, this is what we all personally desire and need at times like this. It's what others need too. When the battle is bigger than the person, that's our cue that the body is being called up to stand with them and fight alongside. That's what "Kingdom family" is for and it's when we are at our best.

Those few days after we were able to get my Mum back to Australia, which let me tell you is no easy journey from the middle of India, were intense. We were praying, decreeing, worshipping, commanding, releasing faith, and trying to enjoy seeing my Mum in the middle of all that, since we'd not seen her much because they lived in India. Mum arrived on a Thursday, was seen by doctors on Friday, admitted to the emergency room on Saturday, and family—my sisters who had not seen Mum in a long time—flew in that weekend. She was diagnosed with terminal cancer Monday and died on Tuesday, still in her 50s. This was incredibly traumatic for everyone and hard to deal with as you can imagine.

A LIFE-CHANGING ENCOUNTER

In the middle of this, God gave me a gift.

Tuesday morning I woke up early, before light, and felt compelled to drive to the hospital and just sit with my Mum praying. I'm glad I did as it was my last time to be alone with my Mum this side of Heaven. She was mostly not aware of my presence and didn't look well, but I sat and quietly prayed and spoke words of life over Mum. Later that morning, Dad and Ben joined me in the hospital. Mum's breathing abruptly changed and the atmosphere shifted in the hospital room. Without a word spoken, all three of us stood up and starting praying out loud. I could feel expectation in the atmosphere, faith even as God's presence was suddenly and tangibly real and close.

Suddenly, I saw an angel *drop* into the hospital room. I was overcome. I yelled out and pointed to the angel, "Dad, there's an angel in the room!" The presence of God was so thick, so overwhelming. I was frozen still. All of us in the room immediately thought that the angel was there to heal Mum. Our prayers became loud and intense in that moment, though I know I became silent as I was suddenly taken into an encounter.

I know I've shared a few angelic encounters in this book. Despite often seeing the supernatural at times, the encounters I've had with my eyes open and seeing into the glory realm with such clarity and "realness" as this have been rare. However, all of these encounters have marked me with increased awe and fear of the Lord.

The Angel Looked Directly at Mum

The angel stood at the end of the hospital bed and stared straight at Mum, who knew the angel was there. It was just taller than Ben, around 7 foot tall, and exuded bright intense light. All his attention was focused on Mum. Suddenly Mum's entire countenance changed, her breathing changed from labored to easy, her skin tone changed from grey to healthy, and her entire body looked suddenly well and normal. She opened her eyes for the first time in a long time and was completely alert as she stared at the angel. Somehow, as can only happen in an encounter God allows, I was completely a part of what was taking place. Faith in the room was off the charts. His glory was felt and was coursing through my body.

Death, Where Is Your Sting

I somehow knew, as only you do in an encounter, that there was some form of communication going on between Mum and the angel. I didn't hear the words of the conversation, but I somehow knew an entire conversation was going on; some of which I was aware of, some I wasn't. Yet I knew that every question, unfinished story, incomplete promise, and all her cares of *this* world were being discussed in great depth that brought peace and resolution.

The entire exchange was deeply full of peace and hope; there was no fear, no pain, no regret. Death wasn't even a thought in this encounter, I felt only *life* and great expectation. Now as I look back, I understand with deeper revelation and understanding the verse, *"Where, O death, is your sting?"* This last moment that we call death, was not tainted by death at all. Death had no voice in this moment, death had no power, only life was present, only Jesus…only expectation. So much hope was present in the entire exchange that even as I watched I still thought Mum was being healed.

I was frozen watching, and I understood not to step forward. I somehow knew I was permitted to observe, but to step any further forward into this encounter was not allowed. I could feel eternity in the room. It felt as if I took one step toward this angel, I would have entered eternity's realm as well.

I felt very deep peace. There was absolutely no fear in my Mum, or me. The entire encounter was the most glorious, beautiful, completely at peace experience. The atmosphere was so supernaturally charged that it made me feel more alive than I had ever felt. It was overwhelmingly "real" and life changing.

For days later, I struggled with feeling like this life wasn't real—eternity seemed more real than real. This *earthly* life felt not real, like a shadow by comparison. It really affected me. Eternity is more real than our short lives here. Heaven is unquestionably a real destination and it is more real than here, more *alive* than what we call alive. There is nothing "less than" about Heaven, it's "more than"—more than we can imagine.

Only in discussion with Ben much later did I discover that the entire encounter had been about one minute long. This completely shocked me; and if not for the fact that I trust Ben, I would have said that was a lie. The encounter I was part of was at minimum twenty minutes, if not hours, as time was somehow timeless, extended, unrushed, unlimited, without end. What I was observing was long, unhurried, two-way conversations that covered so many things and left no question unanswered, no story incomplete. I was taken into a glimpse of eternity's time and it is *not* hurried.

Mum's prayer and faith was that she would be healed and cancer would not take her. I can honestly say that in that moment she was healed and cancer didn't take her; rather, Jesus escorted her to Heaven. Both Ben and Dad saw the profound physical change in her body, and it was this that encouraged them to keep decreeing life as we saw her being healed before our eyes.

Then, suddenly, I sensed all was complete. I remember "knowing" there was a readiness, an expectancy, a surge of hope. I watched my Mum's body shake and I knew she stepped from this life into eternity. The angel immediately disappeared. I looked at Mum and knew she lived somewhere else now, and I knew this was wonderful. Mum was now with Jesus. She's there right now, very much alive as I write this, very fulfilled. There was only life present in her departure from here to her heavenly home. Death didn't have the final say, and that's what impacted me the most.

It's hard to describe because what perhaps should have been the worst moment watching my Mum's physical body die, was actually one of the best memories of my life—thanks only to Jesus—it's the most glorious encounter I've ever had. Mum's going to Heaven was nothing but beautiful, peaceful, and full of God. Even sadness wasn't part of it. The love and presence of God was so thick that only life was present. So much so that even the sting of death wasn't there for me. Praise God, it truly was a precious gift.

There was so much life in the room that even after Mum went to Heaven, we all immediately started praying for resurrection. It was just the obvious reaction and happened without a word spoken. There was complete faith she was coming back. The room was charged with life.

The resuscitation team came in and worked on Mum with no success, and then I asked the head doctor to leave the room as we wanted to pray for resurrection some more, and allow family time to be with Mum, especially my sisters and Dad. We prayed for hours. We owed her that. She didn't come back. I could still feel the effects of eternity in every part of my body...nothing felt real compared to God's glory. I knew beyond a doubt my Mum was completely at peace and alive, I had watched the excitement and peace and resolution of every question unfold in the encounter. My Mum's departure was life giving.

WHEN I DIDN'T UNDERSTAND

The normal sadness of my mum not being "here" anymore was of course really hard, and I had to process that, as we all do. I missed her so much. I still do. Mum had a childlike joy and tenderness, and yet a fierce strength that I still miss. Tears took a while to come, as in the moment there was no grief, no death in that moment. Only hope. Only Jesus.

Eventually though, questions began to take over my heart. I began to get upset that my Mum was no longer here, and the questions I didn't understand started taking over. More to the point, I allowed the things I didn't understand to fester as disappointment. Why was Mum not healed and alive on earth? Why did this happen when my parents had loved so many, healed so many, and had such faith? Why? How come? I didn't understand. Everything I didn't understand began to infiltrate my thinking, and little by little, disappointment in God grew. But slowly, very slowly, so slowly I hadn't even noticed it happening, my heart was growing cold, discontented, and distant from God.

DISAPPOINTMENT IN GOD

I've heard it said, disappointment happens when we hold God hostage to what we told Him to do and how we expected Him to do it. It's holding God captive to our rules of engagement.

I would add to that: disappointment is when we place our desire for understanding before our obedience to trust. It's making an idol of understanding, which actually is what happened in the Garden of Eden all those years ago. The tree of knowledge of good and evil became the disconnection point. "I want to understand so I can trust," while God is asking us to place understanding secondary to trust. And let's face it, until we get to Heaven, there will always be something we don't fully understand.

I want to emphasize that wisdom, understanding, knowledge, and a questioning, curious mind, are all qualities that come from God and are good. It's only when we place them as a prerequisite to our trust in God that we get in trouble and inevitable disappointment starts to simmer.

Months later when, I was in worship at church, the Holy Spirit cut into my thoughts and interrupted. I laugh thinking about that, the Holy Spirit interrupted my worship. I guess if anyone has the right, it's Him! Anyway, the gentle voice of the Holy Spirit asked me a question I will never forget, "Will you still trust Me?" It took me aback. I heard the emotion of God in the question. There was tenderness, love, and—genuine freedom to choose.

But what broke me, and still does thinking about it now, is that I heard the pain in God's question, the sadness of God asking will I still trust Him? I heard nothing but love. There wasn't any anger, there wasn't frustration, there wasn't shame. There was the pain of our once-close hearts being distant. God knew there was a rift, a disconnection on my part—that my heart wasn't as close to Him as I had been. I heard the sadness of my King who desired to hold me and comfort me, and yet I knew—I had a choice. Would I? Would I still trust Him?

As can only happen in a conversation with our King, divine understanding dropped without many words spoken. I suddenly knew I had made "understanding" or more correctly "not under-standing" a prerequisite for my trust in Him. My heart had grown cold because I was choosing understanding above trust, and I'd lost my peace, my joy, and my childlike trust.

I cried a lot of tears in that moment when I realized what I had been doing. I fell on the ground and said how sorry I was. I felt no shame as I knew God understood how I got there, and yet He was gently calling me back to the joy I used to walk in. I felt His soul-quieting, complete love—my always loving Father in Heaven. I surrendered my heart again, and committed to trusting, even where I didn't understand.

I realized I missed my friendship with God. Only months ear-lier He had given me such a gift and allowed me to enter into the most precious moment in my mum's life—leaving this life and going to live in Heaven. Now just months later I found myself doubting if I could trust the King of kings with my heart just because I didn't understand something. It seems ridiculous when I put it like that.

GO BEYOND THE CEILING OF YOUR LAST DISAPPOINTMENT

Disappointment doesn't just disconnect us from God, this same disconnection affects our prayer life and what we're prepared to believe for. We will slowly discover we are backing away from deep connection rather than running toward God's heart, or from attaching our faith to more. We find ourselves living in "comfortable" and retreating from dreaming for more, and not pressing the boundaries of faith and what's possible anymore.

Disappointment traps us in mediocre, safe, and lifeless places where we stop extending our faith for anything big so as not to be "disappointed." But in doing so, we stop really *living*. We condemn our own heart to less than "life, and life abundant" (John 10:10). History is made by those who believe for more than they can currently achieve alone; and this, my friend, means stepping outside comfortable, extending our faith, and going beyond the current ceiling of our last disappointment. You will soar into new realms of trust, and new realms of deep connection with God that open up whole new realms of possibility, when the ceiling of disappointment is smashed. Get ready to soar again into childlike joy.

So yes, God gave me a gift, the gift of renewed childlike trust.

> *And the peace of God, which surpasses all understanding, will guard your hearts and minds through Christ Jesus* (Philippians 4:7 NKJV).

Pastor Bill Johnson says it so well, "If we want the peace that surpasses all understanding, we have to give up our right to understand everything."

Being part of the "moving to eternity" moment with my Mum was a precious gift that has changed how I do life. I already lived to hear those words, *"Well done, good and faithful,"* (Matthew 25:23), but now they are etched into every fiber of my being. Heaven is more real than here, this life—and living with eternity in mind, changes how I live.

Some things matter less, some things matter more. One thing matters the most, have I loved God well today? (and sometimes loving God well is simply loving those around me and seeing them through God's heart). Have I trusted my King, even where I haven't seen the way? Have I remembered today that I'm loved by God, and that one day there's only one thing that will matter—none of the things that bother me now will rate at all. All that will matter is, have I chosen to love and serve my King Jesus in this life, so I can join Him, and those that have gone before me, for all eternity.

THE MOST IMPORTANT PRAYER

I want to take a moment now to pray the most important prayer we can ever pray. I know for many, this story about Mum leaving this life and going to Heaven will have stirred you in the deepest places of your heart. Perhaps you realized disappointment with God has crept into your heart. You may feel compelled to reconnect to God yourself, and so simply pray with me:

> *"Forgive me, Lord, for making understanding a prerequisite for trust and letting my heart grow disconnected from You because of disappointments and*

things I haven't understood. I trust You, God. I surrender my heart and say I trust You even when I don't understand. I ask for my childlike joy to return so we can talk like we used to, Lord. I love You, Jesus. I really need You in my life. I understand that disappointments hurt; and where there has been very real pain, hurt, and loss, I ask You for comfort and to bring divine healing. I ask for Your presence to hold me tight in the places I need a touch from You most. Only You, God, can heal the brokenhearted and the grieving, and I ask for this grace of Yours to come into my heart and life right now."

Or perhaps you are feeling stirred because you know that for the first time, or the first time in a very long time, you are feeling a tug from Heaven to "come *home* to King Jesus" and make Him Lord of your life. Like me, you may have made understanding everything a prerequisite to trusting God, and disappointment has kept you at a distance from Him. You may sense the urgency of "getting your heart right with God" and having assurance that when you leave this life, you too will spend eternity in Heaven. If this is you, friend, would you simply pray with me:

"I'm sorry, God, for holding You captive to my expectations of what You should do and how You should do it before I will trust You. I am sorry for my sins and I receive Your forgiveness, and ask You to take over my life. Thank You for coming into my heart afresh right now. I surrender my life and ask You to be my King, my Savior, and my Friend who is faithful. I receive Your complete love of me, Your mercy, grace, and peace to my soul. I love You, God. Would You fill me with Your Holy Spirit afresh and give me strength and power to live for You. Restore my childlike

joy, comfort me, heal me, and fill me with expectation of the adventures we will enjoy in this life and the next. Thank You, Jesus."

Note: If you prayed that saying yes to Jesus for the first time, we would love to hear from you, friend. You can contact us at www.pouritout.org/yes.

THE KING'S DECREE FOR YOU

"I take away all pain; I have complete peace for you to live in."

—THE KING

MY PRAYER FOR YOU

My friend, I bless your heart to live fully and be comforted in the manifest presence of God. I'm praying right now for an impartation of the awareness of Heaven's reality and how this impacts how we live now. I pray you experience the richness and tenderness of God's tangible nearness today. I bless you with hope in the places you need it most. May you know God's consuming love and live to hear those beautiful words from King Jesus, "Well done, my good and faithful friend." In Jesus' name, amen.

DECREE

- I trust You, God, even when I don't understand or see a way forward.

- I decree disappointment is broken in the name of Jesus.

- My trust is not dependent on my own understanding, but on knowing that You are a good and faithful God.

P.S. This chapter is specifically dedicated to my mum who always wanted to write a book, but was busy saving others' lives with her life. What I'd like to say to you, Mum, "You wrote a book on earth in the hearts of those you loved. I know I wouldn't be me without you, Mum, and not just this book, but my life is still writing pages that your love and prayers are responsible for. I love you, Mum, and miss you. *See you again*, xo."

Chapter 14

BLESSING SMALL
BEGINNINGS

Do not despise these small beginnings....
—ZECHARIAH 4:10 NLT

The Bible says that God completes what He begins: "*being confident of this very thing, that He who has begun a good work in you will complete it until the day of Jesus Christ*" (Philippians 1:6 NKJV).

I also love how The Passion Translation expresses this. I join my faith with yours and decree the same over you. What God has begun, He will continue the process, even adding the finishing touches until He's completed what started as small.

> *I pray with great faith for you, because I'm fully convinced that the One who began this glorious work in you will faithfully continue the process of maturing you and will*

*put his finishing touches to it until the unveiling of our
Lord Jesus Christ!* (Philippians 1:6 TPT)

Blessing small beginnings has been one of the single most valuable and inspiring strategies for me. For anyone who has been "in process" of a miracle, or just going after more, this verse gives not just hope, but divine strategy. Celebration and thanks are powerful tools also. Being thankful positions us to enter more, as it magnifies and sharpens our focus on God. And it honors God.

I will praise the name of God with a song, and will magnify Him with thanksgiving (Psalm 69:30 NKJV).

Eyes that are focused on God will always see something that is worthy of praise. It's why the angels around the throne can say, *"Holy, holy, holy"* (Revelation 4:8) continually, as they keep discovering afresh the manifest beauty and holiness of God! It never grows dull, and clearly they never become so familiar with His presence that it doesn't evoke perpetual awe and wonder. I often imagine these angels in the throne room saying, "Wow, wow, wow!" Our God is worthy of our "Wow!" A childlike heart will always live in wonder and see the perpetual goodness of God that He hides for us to find. Childlike hearts see God through eyes of wonder and they notice things that others don't.

Maturity in the Kingdom was never meant to look like growing out of childlikeness. The more mature we become, the more childlike we should become. Only the voice of a "religious spirit" wants to dampen childlike excitement and wonder in the Kingdom. A normal response to a miracle, for instance, is a thankful, wow God! Familiarity and complacency in the Kingdom are noticed when we are no longer moved by the goodness of God, or see His goodness in our lives in the everyday little kisses from Heaven. Thanking God for the small things is a powerful key to enter into more.

Zechariah 4:10 takes it a step further. This Scripture basically asks, "Who would dare despise something God has done simply because it's a small beginning and not a complete story yet?" Or, who would look down on, sneer at, dislike, loathe, reject, snub, undervalue, or disregard the beginning of something God is doing, just because it's not finished yet?

As we celebrate small beginnings and thank God for them, we can come into agreement with the plan of Heaven and decree completion of what God has just begun. The act of thanking Him for the small change, the little blessing, and the start of breakthrough releases more and is an expression of the working of miracles. When we partner with God and we see the start of breakthrough—that is breakthrough! The start of something is the perfect place to decree and speak life over what God is beginning.

A tool I often use when I'm praying for others or myself is that when I notice any improvement, breakthrough, or any difference, no matter how small, I thank God for it. I then bless it and celebrate as I acknowledge that God completes things He starts. I'm actually coming into agreement with the Holy Spirit when I ask Him for more. I thank God, bless what's begun, and ask for more!

This is how we capture the fullness of a miracle in our spirits before we see its completion in the natural, and activate our faith for more. Whenever I see a miracle or manifestation of glory of any kind, I see it as a promise that there is more available. It's why often some miracles happen in clusters, as people's faith grows for certain miracles as we see something begin to happen in others, and it builds corporate faith.

GOD BLESSES OUR SMALL STEPS

God blesses our small faith steps to believe for more. Every time I hear of something God has done, see something incredible that expands what I will believe for, or hear a testimony of God's goodness, my heart is to take this and use it to grow my faith to carry more in my life. When we steward our small beginnings and live with a heart to honor all that we see God doing in our midst, it brings increase. Small beginnings stewarded well grow hunger for more and position us to carry greater authority.

A few times God has dramatically shown me the importance of blessing small beginnings in some *remarkable* ways. Each of these incredible God stories was the beginning of increased faith and hunger for more:

1. *Two Tiny Diamonds*

When we were moving out of our house years ago in the middle of a hard season, the same house that God saved from foreclosure and right before we went on the road as a family as full-time missionaries, I was furiously cleaning the house. I was doing the final cleaning when Ben phoned and told me some really hard news. It was the backstory of my angelic Justice and Mercy encounter.

It was a hard season and, as mentioned previously, it seemed lots was coming against us. Right after I finished talking to Ben, I was feeling anxious about our new season of stepping out into a new level of faith and needed reassurance from God. I was going through the final inspection before we would walk out of our home into a new season "on the road," and I looked down and saw something shiny on the living room carpet. I thought, *I better pick that up,* and as I reached down to grab it, I couldn't believe my eyes.

There were two little diamonds in the middle of our empty house. They were beautiful and really tiny.

I was amazed as you can imagine and absolutely in awe of God! I picked them up and to be quite vulnerable, I actually thought, *Why are they so tiny?* I'd seen supernatural diamonds before and yet these were so tiny by comparison. I know that's a terrible thought. Well, God hears our thoughts, and I immediately heard the Holy Spirit say right back to my heart, "Do not despise the day of small beginnings!" Um, wow, and ouch.

How kind is God. What an incredible gift and promise before we began a new season that required new faith. If God could do that, He could do everything else I needed too. I still have those two little diamonds, and they have become the most precious of gifts. Remember that God completes what He begins. Actually writing about this brings me to tears. How often I have leaned on this promise in my journey.

2. *Five Little Diamonds in the Pineapple Revival*

In the first week of the Pineapple Revival, five little diamonds dropped all at once and in all different places across the building. What a faith builder for everyone there that night, and a beautiful gift for those who received one of these diamonds. I knew it was a sign that God was with us, and that He would financially provide for the needs of the season we were about to enter into.

I also knew, once again, God was saying, these are small beginnings, Jodie, but bless them and they will grow. Who despises the day of small beginnings? Well that small beginning continued for eighteen months of night after night revival and still continues in the lives of those God blessed, and all God did to impact a nation. It wasn't about the diamonds, it was the hunger, the salvations, the tangible presence and power of God, but this sign and wonder expanded my faith that I could trust Him for everything else. The revival just kept growing and going from glory to glory.

As an aside, something I've discovered about revival is that it often starts small. If we are waiting for the full-blown manifestation of revival before we will recognize the beginning of something unique, we can miss what God is doing in our own backyard and the opportunity to see it grow.

3. Supernatural Honey

Some years ago, Ben and I and our team, including Keely, were in our prayer room planning and dreaming about the next season of Pour It Out. We'd been there for at least an hour, when suddenly there was a rich, strong, sweet smell of honey in the room. None of us had left the room and no one was eating, yet the strong smell of honey was undeniable.

Ben immediately noticed something sticky had appeared on his right arm; and as he touched it, the thick smell of honey infused the entire room. The smell was so strong we felt like we could actually taste it. Just the night before, in our ministry school, Ben had been teaching on the goodness of God in the land of "milk and honey." Well, I knew that honey often represented revelation and healing in the Bible, so I jumped down next to Ben and grabbed a little honey to eat! I mean, I just couldn't help it! I remember thinking, *If that's for healing, I'm having some of that!*

Just a couple weeks later, after a meeting, some of our youth received honey on their arms. Lauren was one of those youths who excitedly came running to show us the supernatural honey that had suddenly appeared. All these years later, she is part of Pour It Out Ministries now. What an incredible sign that God was moving as we planned and dreamed with God. A sign that He was releasing revelation and healing. I also really loved that our youth celebrated a small sign from God, because He is that creative, powerful, and big. And if He can do that *small* thing, He can take care of their lives.

When I see a sign like this, I always think—*If God can make honey manifest, He can certainly make new body parts appear in people, heal incurable diseases, reverse pandemic disease, protect lives, reform laws that deny justice, reverse a nation's economy, bring nation-changing revival, save entire universities, and provide prophetic solutions to the seemingly insolvable problems of our world.* These small beginnings of breakthrough, spark faith in me to believe for more.

4. One Diamond Became Two

The following is another diamond story, which still blows me away. We had been ministering on the Gold Coast of Australia, when a young guy behind us got really excited. A supernatural diamond had appeared on his leg while he worshipped. He was so happy. This young man had been through some challenges, and so it really spoke the heart of God to see the incredible joy this diamond was giving this guy.

Later he was showing it to Keely and I and saying how happy he was. It was a reasonable size diamond. Right in front of our eyes, as both Keely and I watched, the diamond suddenly become two! It didn't split in half. It became two equal-size diamonds, before our eyes. All three of us were watching as the one diamond suddenly became two. We were all amazed at what we just watched happen. What a sign of supernatural increase and multiplication, apart from other things! I'll never forget this. God is the God of creative miracles and multiplication. *If He can make a diamond appear, He can heal mental illness, turn governments back to righteousness, restore honor of unborn life and marriage. He can heal families, find kidnapped children, bring hope to the depressed and freedom to the addict, reverse the suicide epidemic, heal diseases like Alzheimer's and stage four cancer, and find a solution to that problem that weighs heavy on your heart, friend.*

5. Parkinson's Healing

I was praying for a lady a few years ago who was uncontrollably shaking. I will always remember that after about ten minutes of prayer, she slowly started to stand still. As we blessed the small changes we were noticing, the look on her face when she realized she wasn't shaking was priceless. Over the coming year her healing progressed as she, and others continued to bless the small beginnings of healing in her body. Well, not so small really, because when it's your story and it's an incurable disease, every improvement is huge!

Her continual recovery and healing journey has been profound and a recent medical test showed normal functioning. Her decrees as she faithfully continued to speak life over what God began that first night we prayed together remind me that small beginnings prophesy completion!

6. Gold Tears

Ministering in Adelaide, Australia, some years ago, I remember a girl who was visibly upset and struggling. When we invited people to respond for prayer, she immediately came forward. My heart was really drawn to her, and I sensed God was doing a really deep work. From the little she shared, I knew she had been through a really hard season; and as I prayed, she just wept. The presence of God was really sweet and thick, and I was about to leave her as it was obvious that God was really ministering to her and I didn't want to disturb what was going on.

Then I looked at her face, and I saw something incredible start to happen. Where tears were running down her face, I watched gold start to appear. It looked like a thick, metallic gold pen was drawing on her face. Wherever there was a tear, liquid gold was appearing before my eyes on her skin. I was overcome and astounded at the beauty of what was unfolding; I stood back and blessed what God was doing. She was completely unaware as she was deep in an encounter that clearly was ministering to her heart.

What a beautiful sign of what God was doing inside this girl and that God treasures our hearts, heals our pain, and brings beauty from ashes. I was so happy to see her again a week later and shared with her what I saw God doing the week before. She was so incredibly touched by God's tender care and what He began in her life that day, and so was I. I'll never forget seeing those tears becoming liquid gold right before my eyes.

> *You keep track of all my sorrows. You have collected all my tears in your bottle. You have recorded each one in your book* (Psalm 56:8 NLT).

Stories like these make me so happy. I want to see more, I want to know more of the multifaceted beauty, wisdom, and love of God. Lord, I ask for more. *We* ask for more. Every small beginning of breakthrough, every miracle that stretches our hearts, every testimony that makes us say, "Wow God," are faith builders, and equally invitations—for more. Blessing small, being thankful, and decreeing more is powerful. May our voices partner with God as we decree, "More!"

What are the stories in your life where God has already begun doing something new? Bless those small beginnings of change, thank God for all He's currently doing, and ask Him for more.

THE KING'S DECREE FOR YOU

"I have blessed the small beginnings in your life, bless them with me. These small seeds will grow into an abundant harvest. Don't miss what I am doing just because it hasn't grown into fullness yet. Celebrate the small beginnings, for I find great delight in this."
—THE KING

MY PRAYER FOR YOU

I bless your eyes to see with fresh perspective and clarity. I bless you with increased revelation and divine wisdom. I pray that God would give you eyes to see the small starting points of breakthrough in your life in a new way. I bless every small beginning and prophesy completion. I ask for fullness and fruition of every seed, as I bless the miracles God is working in your life right now. I pray for an insatiable, childlike hunger for the things of God and that awe and wonder would rise up in you in fresh ways. I pray for hope to be restored and that you would know God is completing what He has already begun in you. In Jesus' name, amen.

DECREE

- I decree that God completes what He begins!
- I bless what You have planted and speak life to every small beginning.
- I decree the small seeds will grow into a great of harvest.
- I am walking in increasing childlike faith!
- I will use celebration and thankfulness as a tool to position myself for the more.
- I decree that my small beginnings are blessed.

Chapter 15

REVERSING THE HITS OF THE ENEMY

And we know that all things work together
for good to those who love God, to those who
are called according to His purpose.
—ROMANS 8:28 NKJV

I had a profound dream for the Church recently. I saw *"the bride"* on a Ferris wheel without seats, so it required standing and holding on tight. It suddenly sped up really fast. I knew God was saying that the past seasons for many has been like this, going around and around in what has felt like circles, battling many issues that required constant "standing on the Word" to stay on course and believe for breakthrough. The bride has learned to stand on God's promises, and gained strength even as acceleration has come, and holding on was hard. But—it has felt like we haven't moved forward—as we've been busy fighting constant battles.

In the next scene the bride was getting on a roller coaster with no seats! Again, it required standing and holding on tight. Then, just like the Ferris wheel, the roller coaster sped up quickly. It was a wild ride! To stay on the journey—traveling over mountains of incredible beauty, going into deep valleys, unexpected twists and turns, and passing by amazing scenes—required holding on even tighter than the Ferris-wheel-season had, and "standing on the promises of God" was essential, as there were no seats!

When we reached the end of the roller-coaster ride, there was a collective sigh, "Thank goodness we got through that!" It had been a hair-raising journey, but we made it. I was aware "we" had taken ground, however, in the roller-coaster-season as we advanced forward and held on tight to God and decreed truth. Unlike the Ferris wheel, we were not just going around in circles, but had taken new territory, however it hadn't really been fun. Those who had been on the ride were shaken, had grown stronger, elated to have made it—but the journey had taken a toll.

Then suddenly to everyone's surprise, the roller coaster started to move again, except this time the roller coaster was moving in reverse! People were shocked, and were not expecting it to reverse. It sped up, faster than ever. I knew acceleration was upon the bride. As the roller coaster accelerated into reverse, I heard a voice announce loudly, "NOW I AM REVERSING THE EFFECTS OF THE ENEMY'S HITS."

I woke up with great expectation! I understood this was speaking to the body, and God was restoring the toll of the battles of the past seasons on His bride. We are in an era where God is reversing what the enemy has stolen, messed with, and interrupted. The reversal of the hits of the enemy from the journey we have been through will happen suddenly and quickly, and even surprise many. God has seen what the journey cost us and is reversing the effects of the enemy's hits in our lives. God wants His people to know you have gained great strength from the battles, taken new ground, and He's seen your faithfulness to hold on. He will reverse and redeem what the journey had "cost" you.

Let me get real vulnerable quick so I can get to the point in the hope that this encourages you.

One of the surgeries that God used to save my life also caused some horrible issues. This is where I get really vulnerable, but I say this to encourage you. The surgeon accidentally cut a muscle in my intestines that was medically irreversible and in their words "would not heal." This meant I was facing being a level of incontinent for the rest of my life, and I already spent way too much time in the bathroom due to intestinal disease and complications, etc. The day the surgeon told me this, I remember hearing it and saying out loud, "Nothing is impossible with my God," and I meant it. Since this life-saving operation that "went wrong," there were complications that were affecting every facet of my life and were hard to get my head and heart around.

As I drove home from the doctor's office, I had to pull over as sudden sobbing came over me. I just couldn't stop crying. It was like the floodgates opened and every place that had hurt seemed to leak out in an ugly crying session beside the road. I often wonder what passersby thought because this wasn't a quiet cry. It was a wailing. I was tired, hurting, scared, and desperate. This surgery was after God said, "Zerubbabel" to me when my TV "prophesied." It was after the angel stood on the end of our bed and commissioned us into ministry. It was after much supernatural breakthrough already.

This was a "hit" that I was struggling to understand and to get my head around what it really meant for my life moving forward. Nothing made sense to me. I've never doubted God's goodness. I doubted if my faith was strong enough for this challenge. *How could I go on when I thought we had passed this storm already.*

After a long time crying beside the road, I remember suddenly sensing unusual hope begin to arise. My God called me Zerubbabel. My God works all things together for good, including the things that aren't good. My God is the God of all things are possible, which includes the things I think are impossible. I decreed "reversal" over and over.

YOU WON'T EVEN SMELL LIKE SMOKE

"Look!" he answered, "I see four men loose, walking in the midst of the fire; and they are not hurt, and the form of the fourth is like the **Son of God"** *(Daniel 3:25 NKJV).*

All the important people, the government leaders and king's counselors, gathered around to examine them and discovered that the fire hadn't so much as touched the three men—not a hair singed, not a scorch mark on their clothes, not even the smell of fire on them! (Daniel 3:27 The Message)

The Bible story in Daniel, of the rescue of Shadrach, Meshach, and Abednego is one of my favorites. Three young Hebrew men who refused to worship any other god than the one true God were sentenced to death and then miraculously rescued by *"the Son of God!"* That's amazing right there—Jesus was making a guest appearance! The Bible tells us that after the boys were rescued, God so reversed the effects of the fire that was designed to kill them, that not even a hair was burnt and their clothes didn't even smell of smoke!

Then Nebuchadnezzar, the king, instituted a nationwide governmental honor of the one true God as King—sounds like national revival—and promotes all three young men, reversing the previous orders! What a turnaround. Not only did God save them, but He reversed the effects of the enemy's hits so much so they were now promoted.

The "smell" of the past season's attacks and fires of persecution were removed from them, and an entire region was impacted and influenced by the notable miracle of reversal and their faith! It's easy to read these stories and not think about how it felt to think you're losing your life, go through the entire traumatic ordeal of being thrown into the actual fire, and then living to tell the tale. They had a legitimate story of God's saving, redemptive power in the middle of catastrophic circumstances. God was with them throughout the entire ordeal and ensured they were unharmed by what the enemy threw at them.

This is your promise from God as well. Not only has God rescued His bride from the blazing fire, but God is reversing even the effects of the battle where it's taken a toll on His people. You don't just walk free when God redeems, you walk out with promotion, added influence, and reversal of the enemy's schemes against you. I want you to get this—your promise is that even the effects of the fire are being reversed. You won't carry the residue with you for the rest of your life of what you walked through. Now that's incredible. That's our God. That's redemption right there. Reversing not just the curse, but even the effects of the hits of the enemy. God is giving it all back, including those years the locust ate (Joel 2:25). Yes, God is even redeeming the time lost.

WORKING ALL THINGS TOGETHER

Many wonder how God can redeem lost years or make up time that was seemingly ravaged by the enemy, or at the least held people captive in perpetual delay. Romans 8:28 is my go-to promise for holding on to truth to reverse the effects of what you've walked through. It's a Romans 8:28 season. So many have walked through enemy assault and what can only be best described as an onslaught of "stuff" coming from every side. *But,* we will watch and see God redeem our stories and promises, as well as reverse the effects that walking through the "valley of the shadow of death" caused. And just as in my dream, for many, this will happen *suddenly and fast.*

> *And we know that all things work together for good to those who love God, to those who are called according to His purpose* (Romans 8:28 NKJV).

This verse has been like a friend. Often, even as we "get the breakthrough," we are left with effects of the season that are a residue of the fire we've come through. This is where I've decreed Romans 8:28 over and over as my inheritance.

"I will not even smell of smoke. I will carry the fragrance of having been with Jesus!" That's a decree to carry in your heart too.

Let me tell you, there has been some "residue" in my life of battles I've journeyed through, that needed a Romans 8:28 do-over. Having faced multiple health challenges and lived feeling unwell has left an emotional, physical, and spiritual residue that I had to face, decree truth to, and deliberately walk free from. I had to learn *how* to *think* like a well person and make decisions based on faith, not fear. I had to learn how to *choose* to thrive and not just survive. How to live in rest, and yet equally live in trust so that I choose to "do" my life even in less-than-perfect conditions—trusting God to make up the difference.

I think this resonates with everyone, as we all face the same questions, just in different capacities and situations. We have to trust God to be our everything and that He will work things together for good in the midst of the "not good." Courage in the face of things that scare us—this is God's gift to trusting hearts.

For months after the muscle was accidentally cut during surgery, I decreed Romans 8:28 and slowly this damaged muscle miraculously improved and healed a great deal. *Praise God!* It was an emotional, painful, and often *very* embarrassing journey at times. I did the only thing I could do though, I held on to God's Word and walked in grace for my day while stirring up hope that pain was not my future. Leaning into God's hope was essential, because my hope would run out, but His hope never did, and never does. The same is true of faith, God's faithfulness is perpetual, boundless, and never runs out.

After a great deal of healing that astounded doctors, this particular muscle and situation seemed to stall in recovery. There's been a process of continued prayer and pressing in that's required ongoing faith to walk out. Not everything healed quickly; there are some things still in process even as I write this. But God doesn't half-do jobs; as we know, what He starts He completes. This is a promise to be held on to and decreed.

Jeremiah 30:17 (NKJV) is a great verse to decree too: *"For I will restore health to you and heal you of your wounds,' says the Lord...."*

It is not just health God is restoring—He is healing our wounds too. That means the effects of the hits, the places in us that need reversal of the residue of the journey. Wounds aren't just physical. Any place we need wholeness, God is reversing the effects of the battle. I had to hold on to the reversal word and trust that God works all things together for good.

Not too long before God called us to the United States, I once again needed to go back to the hospital emergency room, as suddenly things were *not good*. A little more vulnerability… To save my life, an emergency operation was necessary to insert a stoma or colostomy bag, which is a removable and disposable bag used to collect waste from the body. I was told this may not work due to so much inflammation in my intestines and the "irreversible mess," as they described it, inside me. Again, we were fighting for my life But the surgery was urgent and saved my life, praise God.

Honestly though, I was devastated as I had been believing this wouldn't happen for twenty-five-plus years, and dealing with "feeling like a failure" and disappointment. God was gracious and gave me incredible peace, even excitement actually. I knew God was with me, close and doing something. There were *many* complications and many calls to prayer for which I'm so incredibly thankful to the many thousands who prayed for me. Prayer literally saved my life many times; but the battle had been intense and seemingly never-ending, with twists and turns I hadn't expected—not unlike the dream of the roller coaster.

When my health situation settled, God said, "Move to America." What!? We knew the call was urgent and it was now or never, and was confirmed by several respected apostolic leaders in Australia and the United States. So as to trust and obey, we made plans, packed up our lives, God opened miraculous doors, and we faithfully and joyfully walked through them—by faith. It was a big deal of trusting God moving to the US, especially with what "they" said was an irreversible stoma bag, which had kept me "bound" to Australia at this point for ongoing medical treatment and supplies.

But God had spoken and very clearly said, "Reversal." There had been a great deal of miraculous, accelerated healing, and suddenly in the midst of so much change, the doctors incredibly changed their diagnosis to, *"No active disease!"* This was a miracle! I was so happy! Then the doctors *reversed* their original decision and said, "We can now reverse the irreversible." Thank You, Jesus! God is sooooooo good!

Oftentimes our lives become a prophetic signpost of what God is doing in the spiritual. This has often been the case for my life. After moving and living in America for a few short months, I returned to Australia for the reversal surgery. However, the reversal process was not straightforward.

I was in and out of the hospital, mostly in, for the better part of four months with allergic reactions to medicine, surgery complications, and infections. What should have been a simple reversal surgery became fighting for my life, and once again many began to pray. After the operation, my body didn't work; it had gone into shock and was not "remembering" how to function normally. I was in extreme pain, confined to bed (and Australia) for four months straight. I knew much depended on a "successful" outcome. I cried every day. I prayed, mostly through tears, and I decreed over and over, "You are reversing the effects of the enemy's hits, I will walk in wholeness. These attacks will stop." I was now without the stoma bag which was a huge miracle, but now my body was worse than it had ever been, and I was literally in the bathroom forty-plus times a day, bleeding, and in pain. I have a high threshold of pain, but I was in pain!

As a further blow, the muscle that had previously been damaged accidentally was further damaged in this surgery, and now I needed to believe for this to heal, again! Crazy, I know. I was distraught at times. I had constant reaction to medicines, so I also couldn't take most pain medication and this was adding to the trauma. However, I did what I knew to do, usually in pain, I would march around the bedroom in tiny shuffles, decreeing God's word. I stood on the truth. I stood on the promises of God. I held on tight to every word God had spoken. God was reversing all the enemy had stolen from me and I was taking it back, even if there had been some unexpected twists and turns.

I understand for many who will read this, sometimes in your life the battle seems intense and never-ending. It would seem often the battle is most intense right before the greatest of breakthroughs. I want to encourage you—where the battle has been the greatest, the God of breakthrough is fighting for you. The enemy and your circumstances don't get to prophesy your future, only God has that role, and His word is clear—all things working together for *good*, not harm. I decree increasing breakthrough over you even right now in the mighty name of Jesus.

This was the hardest of all the battles I had ever walked through in my body. *It was also the last!* I'm not sure why, but it felt like I was fighting for not just my life, but the breakthroughs of others that would follow. Remember, we had no home in Australia as we gave that up to move to the US, so we were with our dear friends John and Jenny, also Pour It Out pastors, who were incredibly gracious to let us stay. But I was going through all this without a home, and now without a country, as I felt caught between two nations—transition can look messy.

Keely and Lauren eventually needed to return to America. It was really hard to say goodbye to them without knowing when Ben and I could return. What was meant to be a relatively simple four-week turnaround, turned into a long five months.

A difficult aspect of this hospital stay was that I hadn't had an encounter this time. I wondered why I hadn't "seen" Jesus like other times of battle in the hospital. Please know God was close, I felt Him very near. It had just been different though, more challenging maybe. Our friend Shawn Bolz later prophesied and told us he had prayed I wouldn't have an encounter as he *knew* as he prayed that if I "saw Jesus" I wasn't coming back. Wow, yes, I cried as the weightiness of that hit me. God saved me. And Jesus is very, very kind.

DESTINY PROMISES

Toward the end of the five months stuck in a bed, I signed the contract to write this book you're reading now, being published by Destiny Image. If there ever was a sign of prophetic destiny promises, for me, this was it. God is reversing the effects of the enemy's hits, redeeming what the enemy stole, and working all things together for good, for me and for *you*. This is for the body of Christ, for all of us. For so many, the last season you've walked out of has left a residue, but God is reversing this in our lives. We are coming out of the fire with promotion and upgrades, and revival fire will be our reward.

When I was finally well enough to board a plane and return to my new home in America, where God had sent us, the place of our new adventure in God, I can't tell you how much I cried because of what it represented. When I got off that plane with the operation reversed and no active disease in my body, I knew once again that my King is my dearest Friend who means it when He says, "I'm with you." He knows what our promises are and He's releasing breakthrough and redemption right where we need it.

Reversal Miracles

In this past season, I've seen so many miracles that have spoken the heart of God to not just bring breakthrough, but reverse the residue. The following are some of those recent miracles.

Self-Harm Scars Gone

A girl who had self-harmed came to one of our meetings and I sensed the presence of an angel behind her, and I prophesied freedom to her. By the end of the meeting, she was visibly different and reconnected to God. A week later, she attended another meeting excited to show us what God did in her. She showed us her arm and revealed where God had removed the scars where she had cut herself. There was only one tiny, faint mark left there that was barely visible. Wow, praise God. Not only did He meet her heart and love her to life, He literally reversed and removed the scars of a past season!

Stage 4 Cancer Diagnosis Reversed

We also prayed for a lady who didn't need to tell us she was unwell, we could see that. She had been diagnosed with stage 4 cancer. She came to the altar boldly for prayer even before I had asked for those who needed prayer. I was moved by compassion for her. A couple of months later we were told by the pastor of the church that this lady's doctors were astounded at the change in her, and that her treatment shrunk the tumors and she suddenly started getting well. They changed her prognosis from dying to, "You will live a full life!" A full reversal of her condition and prognosis took place. Praise God!

As a side note, ever since Mum went to Heaven, I have had a personal decree to see cancer healed, especially stage 4 cases. Praise God. We, and the body, are seeing an increase of cancer healed.

Nine Babies Lost, Broken Marriage, and God's Restoration

As I wrote this chapter, I received an incredible testimony from a lady I prayed for a few years ago in Houston, Texas. She had sadly lost eight babies, and shared how her ninth pregnancy had made it to twenty-four weeks. The baby was born and lived for just over an hour. This was going to be her last try at having a baby, as during this time she and her husband separated.

Days after leaving the hospital without a child, she attended a church where Ben and I were ministering. She was struggling with so much and didn't want to be there, but came up for prayer anyway. I prophesied that God was restoring her family, which she wondered how. I didn't know that at the time they were separated and living in different homes. She said that on the day the divorce papers were delivered, she found out she was pregnant— and miraculously she carried this child full term. Her marriage was restored and they moved into a new home together when their child was five months old. God not only restored their marriage, home, and family, He gave them a healthy child they didn't expect they would ever have.

Dreams Fulfilled

One of God's promises I speak out is that "I'm called to the nations, Lord." Fulfilling that promise of His, I was blessed to travel for ministry to South Africa, Taiwan, Germany, Italy, France, Switzerland, Australia, New Zealand, and all across America— some thirty-plus states and counting. What is miraculous about this, is that it all took place in an eighteen-month season post the reversal surgery and being diagnosed, "No active disease"! Every person I share God's heart with and every nation or new place my feet touched, was and is a praise-worthy shout of thanks to the God of the impossible! That's a quick-reversal God!

Far from saying this to brag about the places I've been, I'm saying this to brag on Jesus, because I remember how I was unable to get out of bed and leave the room, let alone fly to the other side of the world for Jesus! What an honor! He is the God of break-through. For God to redeem so much so quickly, He is worthy of my constant praise. I am thankful to have come through the fire; we serve such an incredible God who wants to even remove and reverse the smell of the smoke as well. Wow God, You are worthy of my stand-and-applause wildly kind of praise! It hasn't always been an easy journey, but it has been a profoundly supernatural journey of increasing breakthrough and miraculous, incredible reversal of the hits of the enemy.

Everyone has walked through tough times. And everyone needs to know God is working all things together for good, even when things have *not* been good and loss or interrupted dreams have marked the past season. Always remember, God is a hope-restorer, working all the details together for good in your life, and redeeming your future story with the joy of not just walking out of the fire, but walking out with the "smell of smoke" reversed and new stories that redeem all that was lost.

The purpose of being vulnerable about my journey into break-through is to impart hope to you that even if the battle has been intense and seemingly continuous for you, your faithful standing and holding on to truth has and *is* shifting things. I don't have answers for why some battles are sometimes difficult, but I do know God's Word stands true, is active and alive, and God is moving in your circumstances.

I want you to know that the dream shared at the start of this chapter is specifically a word to those who have experienced intense warfare and the battle has cost you. It is a word to those who fought and battled and courageously keep believing in the midst of a very *real* journey that God *is* reversing the effects of the hits of the enemy in *real* circumstances and real journeys.

I decree this for you. The enemy's best attempts to stop you advancing have not succeeded—you have taken ground. Not only will you advance farther, quick and sudden breakthroughs will make up even time stolen from you.

This has been a challenging chapter to write because it was a challenging season to walk through—but it makes the victory sweeter. If you are reading this and find yourself in similar circumstances, first of all I want to honor your courage. I want you to know I'm praying for you right *now* and releasing breakthrough. I add my faith to your faith and I call in miracle turnarounds. I speak a shift in your circumstances, peace to the storm, miracles, and reversal of every hit of the enemy, and God's presence to be tangibly near, in Jesus' name. Amen.

Note: Upon finishing writing this, we literally anointed the pages of this chapter with oil believing for your breakthrough.

THE KING'S DECREE FOR YOU

"My child, I love how you love Me. You are called according to My purpose and I make all things work together for your good, even the things that look like they could never be turned around. I am redeeming all things."

—THE KING

MY PRAYER FOR YOU

I pray this over you—God is bringing good into your life, especially where the enemy has stolen from you. I decree, your story is being rewritten with the redemptive blood of Jesus and I ask for an impartation for faith. I decree that God is removing all the residue of walking through the fire and reversing the effects of the hits of the enemy. I bless you with promotion, upgrades, redemption, and astounding breakthroughs. I bless you abundantly with all God has for you, in Jesus' name. Amen.

DECREE

- All things are being worked together for good for me, including the things that were not good.

- Any residue from the battles I have faced is reversed, removed, and redeemed, in Your presence, Lord.

- God doesn't just rescue me from the fire, He completely restores me.

- God is reversing the effects of the enemy's best efforts to stop me from progressing. I will walk in upgrades, increased influence, and promotion.

Chapter 16

THE DREAM CODE

This is what God says, the God who builds a road right through the ocean, who carves a path through pounding waves, the God who summons horses and chariots and armies—they lie down and then can't get up; they're snuffed out like so many candles: forget about what's happened; don't keep going over old history. Be alert, be present. I'm about to do something brand-new. It's bursting out! Don't you see it? There it is! I'm making a road through the desert, rivers in the badlands. Wild animals will say "Thank you!"—the coyotes and the buzzards—because I provided water in the desert, rivers through the sun-baked earth, drinking water for the people I chose, the people I made especially for myself, a people custom-made to praise me.
—Isaiah 43:16-21 The Message

Dreaming helps us formulate new strategies and allows for maximum capacity of creativity as we pursue new "frontiers." We will pioneer and take new territory in the spirit in this new era and in the natural. It's time to dream with abandon once more and stir hope for what is yet possible, and build what hasn't yet existed. Dreaming doesn't just activate hope and provoke creative juices, it stirs faith to go where we've never been before.

It doesn't take a prophet to know that the world is in a season of rapid change. As things shift and change, God is compelling His people to prophesy and decree what He is saying. He wants us to partner with Him to establish on the earth the dreams and plans of Heaven, as we, the body of Christ on earth, are called to pioneer change and extend into new territory. We are being invited to walk in something fresh, something brand-new—and it's time to dream again!

A DREAM ABOUT DREAMING

When I was in Italy, I had a powerful dream that ironically was about dreaming. I was standing in a field, which represents the harvest, and I saw placed in my hand a new, ultramodern, handheld technology that I did not recognize but knew was cutting edge and an extremely helpful tool used for the harvest. It was also very cool looking! It contained new strategic wisdom, fresh blueprints, divine revelation, and pioneering thinking that brought breakthrough for a new era, and helped fast-track vital information. I also knew the purpose of this device and technology was to help win the harvest, and it contained *new*, innovative downloads that unlocked harvest. This wasn't an upgraded version of the old, it was something new. I wanted it! What a gift!

The device required a code though, to gain access to the revelation it held, and I didn't have the code! As I was desperately trying to work out the password to gain access to all this revelation, wisdom, and breakthrough, a hand suddenly appeared in front of me and I was given a handwritten note. The note clearly said, "THE CODE IS DREAM." Then I woke up.

I knew right away the access code, or password, was *dream* to enter the fullness of all God has available in this era. Fresh strategy, energy, revelation, and anointed wisdom is required for this next season as we haven't walked this path before. Stirring not just fresh ideas, but fresh perspective and creative new thinking processes were required because God is releasing new breakthrough advances that are revolutionary game-changers, and not just upgrades of past innovations. To access this new wineskin, dreaming is essential. It isn't just good practice to dream, imagine, and envision right now, *it is imperative* for God's people, as God is reinventing, renewing, recalibrating, and reworking a custom-made wineskin for this era. The prophetic "imagineers" will pioneer a creative reformation. I realized God was saying that to take new territory *required* His people to dream again.

Many have felt the recalibration of this season as God has made room for the new. God has been removing the "unnecessary" to make space for fresh strategies that will unlock greater breakthrough. New frontiers in the spirit are before us, which require an upgraded pioneering spirit that revels in establishing the new, decreeing solutions, and building new wineskin structures of possibility capable of stewarding accelerated change and harvest. It was important to *make room* for something new in our thinking, hearts, and practices.

Many have felt shut down or sluggish in their capacity to dream because of hope deferred, disappointments, and stagnate seasons. God is reactivating the pioneering spirit and creative capacity within His people. You will dream with abandon and build with fresh revelation.

The Church has been walking through a season of transition from one wineskin to a greater-glory wineskin, ready to steward a greater capacity than we have before. The new wine is potent, intense, and explosively powerful—there has been a consecration of our hearts taking place so we can steward what is about to be poured in and out of us.

God doesn't want us to collapse under the increased weight of His intensifying glory; rather He wants us to administer it in new authority and power. It was interesting I had this dream in Italy as one of the purposes of this ministry trip was to dream again. The whole particular trip to Europe was a re-set for Ben and me, as we were entering a new season. It was a time to recalibrate, re-envision, and build a new wineskin for a new season.

As we had recently moved from Australia to the US, it was a time of leaning in for fresh strategy and fresh oil. After this dream, on closer inspection of my own heart, I realized that there were areas in my thinking that past disappointments, or longevity of the battle, had put a ceiling on my ability to dream and hope. Perceived failures, disappointments, and battle weariness had dampened passion and expectation of profound good. Some areas in my heart needed a hope upgrade.

In fact, like many in the body who have walked through delay and prolonged challenges, many are living with not just a hope deficit, but a hope avoidance. This made positioning and planning for the "new" almost impossible as our expectation of good has been minimized, or completely exhausted. We have learned to keep our expectations in check and within "doable" borders, not allowing the thrill of imagining and dreaming with God for fear of further disappointment. Essentially, this has shut down hope, which stifles creativity and puts a cap on breakthrough. It squashes our heart, and takes the joy out of the journey.

The solution for kick-starting our hearts? It's time to dream again. Dreaming with childlike abandon and bubbling expectation stirs passion. Our hearts *will* come alive as we dream on purpose, dream with bubbling joy, dream as warfare, dream for fun, dream just to stir our imagination, and dream as declaration—we must dream again.

We are in a season of accelerated change, and new frontiers of possibility and potential are needed in every sphere of society as our current paradigm of "normal" and "possible" is extended and expanded. Faith expectations are being upgraded and stretched. It's essential to dream and imagine new possibilities and expanded faith frontiers and "see" yourself achieving things you previously thought impossible. Creativity is key to supernatural answers, solutions, and breakthroughs we've never seen before.

Imagine if. Imagine how. Imagine what could be. There are fresh strategies, revelation, and creative miracles to be released we haven't even begun to imagine are possible yet. We need to stretch our capacity to dream and decree what's possible.

Dreaming is restoring your passion, your creative edge, your heart, your hope, and your voice. There's an invitation to lay aside past disappointments, failures, staleness, and things that didn't happen as you'd hoped, and simply dream again. Hope again. Let Jesus restore your spark and unique pioneering spirit, as the act of dreaming stimulates your capacity for new and even affects how we pray. Our prayers and declarations need to reflect the God of "infinitely more."

*Never doubt God's mighty power to work in you and accomplish all this. He will achieve infinitely more than your greatest request, your most unbelievable dream, and exceeded your wildest imagination! He will outdo them all, for **His miraculous power constantly energizes you*** (Ephesians 3:20 TPT).

DRESSED AND READY

There's an *intercession revolution* taking place right now, and your decrees are paving the way for something we have never experienced. We *must* dream again, and let our decrees be saturated in hope and prophetic solutions birthed from the glory realm of "infinitely more." Our voices *must* establish the new era we are entering.

In many ways, we are being dressed in new, custom-made clothes that perfectly fit the season. The sense many have of ill-fitting clothes that belong to a season that is finished, is from the Lord, because the era *has* changed. The sense of displacement and that last season's strategies don't fit anymore is because that is literally the case. The enemy wants you to feel rejected and demoted; but instead, it's the past-season wineskin that is being discarded, and the sense of displacement is the sign to you that you are being promoted into a custom-made wineskin. God is expanding the borders of your influence and releasing strategic wisdom and revelation designed for maximum capacity, maximum potential, and maximum fruitfulness. The body of Christ is being positioned for maximum harvest as our decrees partner with Heaven's heart. The problems of this current generation are *not* too big or beyond redemption, as God is releasing a custom-built wineskin of potent power, glory, and solutions designed especially for *now*.

Now you're dressed in a new wardrobe. Every item of your new way of life is custom-made by the Creator, with his label on it. All the old fashions are now obsolete (Colossians 3:10 The Message).

Ask yourself, *What does my "new wardrobe" look like in this season?* As God is upgrading, anointing, and releasing strategy and tools for maximum impact, ask yourself what is now unhelpful and what is being added? Our new "wineskin" is custom-made by the Creator; allow Him to stretch you, recalibrate, and re-infuse you with freshness. I think we can agree that we are entering a new era, not just a new season; so it's important to decree into the new as our faith declarations establish destiny-producing fertile territory. Establish your new season with decrees that build a framework of "anything is possible with God."

Take a moment with a *great, great is important,* cup of coffee or tea and write down some dreams and decrees to speak over the next decade. What are you seeding into the spiritual ground around you with *your* voice? What are you speaking forth over the new? What are you telling yourself about your season? What faith-expanding prayers are you believing for your sphere of influence and family? Let's speak hope into the future and creative possibility becoming reality.

DOORWAY TO DESTINY BREAKTHROUGH

I had a powerful vision in worship a while ago that speaks to the bride, the Church, as we enter a new era. I saw "the bride" walking up to a door. Over the door was written "DESTINY BREAKTHROUGH." The door was wooden, rustic, and very humble looking. It was also tall and notably *very* narrow. The bride was holding in each hand two suitcases. As she walked toward the narrow door, I watched as she tried to fit through the door as she knew that what was on the other side, was fruitful, fulfilling and what she was made for.

But try as she might, no matter which way she tried to fit through the door, she could not get through the narrow door while still holding on to her suitcases. Even dropping one of the suitcases didn't work as the door was extremely narrow and only just fit the bride herself. There was a sudden awareness that to enter the days of destiny that awaits the bride, she must drop the baggage of the last seasons. All the disappointments, unrealized dreams, offenses, unforgiveness, hidden agendas, unhealthy thinking, even the hurt of loss or fear of failure, anything unhelpful in our connection to God that we, the bride, were holding on to—it all had to be surrendered to walk through the door into the era of destiny breakthrough.

To let go of the baggage, and *all* the baggage, not just some of it, required humility and vulnerability. It required trust to walk through that door—just *you* and God, nothing else.

SWIFT ACCELERATION ENCOUNTER

Around the same time when I saw this vision of the bride, I was awakened in the night by an encounter of something brushing against my arm. As I opened my eyes, I saw a vision of a streak of bronze-like golden light rush by me, so fast I could barely see it. I understood immediately this was a release of "swift acceleration" and that something angelic had just visited me. There was an immediate sense of "change has come." I knew God was releasing swift acceleration upon the Church body and turning things around to be right side up, *swiftly* in front of our eyes.

There's no need to fear the change that is unfolding; for those surrendered to God, it is the breakthrough season we've been decreeing. Things are happening quickly, so it's important to stay focused on God. When acceleration and change are being released, we need to remain focused on what matters, so that we are found running in the right direction. Focus determines direction. When God-change is happening, our decrees are imperative. Our voices become the rudder setting the direction to head in and establish new territory. This is a time to declare what God is saying, and declare with maximum faith, as we are entering the days of greater glory and maximum, unprecedented harvest.

There are rivers being made in the wasteland and roads in the desert by your decrees. We must stop wasting time going over old history and be alert to the brand-new that is bursting out.

> *Forget about what's happened; don't keep going over old history. Be alert, be present. I'm about to do something brand-new. It's bursting out! Don't you see it? There it is! I'm making a road through the desert, rivers in the badlands* (Isaiah 43:19 The Message).

ALIGNMENT ENCOUNTER

Not long after that encounter, I was in Moravian Falls, North Carolina, and I had another significant encounter—this time about alignment.

I got up early in the morning to pray and sensed God telling me to go and stand on the back verandah that overlooks the valley and forest. As I stood there, I had a sense of expectancy that God wanted to show me something. Then, as I looked, I saw a vision, a light that looked like an angel, standing by one of the tallest trees. It was very tall, extremely skinny and narrow, and very bright. It almost looked like a beam of light that was completely straight, and reminded me of a measuring stick. I heard the Lord say it was Alignment and a fresh release of Kingdom alignment was upon the Church body.

I understood God was reestablishing a plumb line of holiness and positioning people for breakthrough and destiny. God is refocusing our vision to see with greater clarity and aligning us to the promise and the King's decree and mandate for this urgent hour. God is releasing breakthrough over your destiny.

There was also an urgency to being aligned to God's heart and being the King's decree for the season. God's heart is beating for the harvest and souls, and this is an urgent decree to win souls. These are the days of greater glory, which means greater harvest. A great awakening of revival glory will win the billions and answer the cry of His people for breakthrough. *The Holy Spirit is aligning us to the decrees of the King.* What His heart burns for, our hearts will burn for too.

It occurred to me as I wrote this, that the vision of Alignment was tall and very narrow, not unlike the vision of the tall and narrow door I saw that the bride was being invited to walk through into destiny breakthrough. She had to drop the baggage to enter into the new. Alignment comes from humility as we surrender and trust God, stepping into the unknown. It reminds me of this poignant Scripture:

> *Come to God through the narrow gate, because the wide gate and broad path is the way that leads to destruction—nearly everyone chooses that crowded road! The narrow*

gate and the difficult way leads to eternal life—so few even find it! (Matthew 7:13-14 TPT)

Suddenlies are upon the body. It is really important in times of acceleration, alignment, and change that we *decree a thing and it shall be established.* Things are happening quickly. It's time to dream again, hope again, and decree. God is accelerating and aligning your destiny promises and bringing harvest breakthroughs in the nations.

Let your heart dream again, as every new breakthrough begins as a dream that someone dared to pioneer.

THE KING'S DECREE FOR YOU

"I have prepared a path for you. I have creative solutions, new ideas, and new pathways of thinking. There is no limit to Kingdom creativity, so keep dreaming, My child. Dream even bigger than you have before. I have heavenly blueprints just waiting for you to engage your faith and dream again."
—THE KING

MY PRAYER FOR YOU

I'm blessing you to dream again, hope again, thrive again, build again, and enter into new territory. I pray blessing over your creativity and a fresh release of Heaven's strategies for the new. I decree change has come to every area of your life that God is realigning and that swift acceleration is upon your promises.

As I'm praying for you right now, I ask the Lord to bless you as you let go of all that is unnecessary and unhelpful as you move into new strategy and breakthrough. I'm blessing you to dream with the Lord of the remarkable days that you are journeying into. I pray God's mighty power in you to achieve infinitely more than your wildest imagination. I decree impartation to pioneer, establish new breakthroughs, and dream the dreams of God on the earth. In Jesus' name, amen.

DECREE

- I decree I will dream again, with bubbling joy!
- I am dressed and ready for the new things God is releasing.
- I am a catalyst of God-change and restoration.
- I am a pioneer of the dreams of God in my sphere of influence.

Chapter 17

DIVINE PAYBACK

But if he is caught, he must pay back seven times what
he stole, even if he has to sell everything in his house.
—Proverbs 6:31 NLT

Divine payback as I call it, is our ultimate redemptive promise.
When we realize what the devil has stolen from us, we can call
back seven times what has been taken. Seven, as defined by the
Bible, implies "fullness, completion, divine perfection." When I
got ahold of what this verse was actually promising, it impacted
and shaped my life in such profound and practical ways —and I
know it will for you as well.

God is never the author of destruction, that is always the work
of the enemy. John 10:10 makes it very clear who authors what.
God always comes to add life—abundant life. The devil comes to
steal, kill, and destroy. It's important to attribute blame in the right

direction. God is good, always. The things that have harmed you and have been stolen from you carry the hallmark of the thief. God is the Redeemer.

When God restores and redeems, He restores the fullness of what the enemy messed with and robbed from you. God's divine payback is upgraded completion. He doesn't give the same back, He restores better than it was before. Simply put, all that the devil has stolen, messed with, broken, destroyed, taken, hijacked, and robbed from you—God redeems and gives back better. Promotion, upgrade and increase are released through divine payback. Divine payback doesn't just give back, it's God's justice system of redemptive favor, supernatural breakthrough, divine upgrades and promotions. I mean come on—what a King we serve!

You are called to be a mighty champion who sets the captives free in the very areas where the enemy wanted to imprison you. I call in increase of healing anointing as my divine payback all the time. Specifically with intestinal, bowel issues, and medically incurable diseases, I call in increased breakthrough.

Where the enemy has intended to harm and rob you, I call back a fullness of redemption and increase over your life. You will walk in authority in the very places the thief thought he won. You, yes *you* are called, anointed, and appointed to release a mighty, redemptive breakthrough.

What has threatened to be the breaking of you, becomes the making of you in the glory. Jesus' blood poured out makes all the difference. Our King Jesus has made a way for divine payback. The "payback" is not about people, it's aimed at the true enemy of our souls. This is your divine inheritance. You will increasingly bring freedom to others in the very places that have threatened to be your demise. God is the great Redeemer.

Where has the thief, the devil, stolen from you? Take a mental inventory and call in divine payback. Your journey is different from mine, but we all have a journey, and we all have places where the thief has stolen from us. For some it is finances or creative flow for wealth creation. For others it's relationships and family connection, or fears and insecurities that have plagued and stifled your call. For some it may have been a constant assault designed to keep you from living victoriously, or to keep you in damage-control mode rather than rising as a breaker of chains and disturber of darkness.

Many have God-dreams that the enemy has torn down with the intent that you won't get back up and build again. The thief will not win. You will not just walk in your breakthrough, you will be a releaser of breakthrough, because behind your breakthrough is a vast harvest of breakthroughs that have been bought with the blood of Jesus. The private "cost" that none have seen is recorded in Heaven as God has seen you. The King decrees it's divine payback time for His people. You will walk in greater authority than before and be part of the solution God is raising up.

I often ask the Lord and decree increased authority in the areas where I've been robbed. I expect increase. And I expect to release this to others. I thank God for completion of redemption and receive anointing for breakthrough on purpose, as my inheritance. I release the same over you.

One area in particular the thief has tried to keep me "hostage" is in bathrooms. As you are aware, I have spent *way* too much time in bathrooms because of physical health challenges and have found myself "stuck" in this area of my life; *so as warfare,* I started decreeing healing and God encounters in every bathroom I entered. I pray, "Touch every person in here, God. Pour out healing, salvation, and sudden revelation of Your goodness that takes people who walk in here by surprise! Heal people, Lord. Speak to people in here, God."

I decided to use the "time" in bathrooms to intercede for breakthrough—especially if the enemy was trying to tell me things would never change. I decree, "Life follows me wherever I go and impacts others around me, including in bathrooms." I know this sounds strange, funny even, but it's true. I decided that if the thief had tried to stop me by keeping me in bathrooms, I was going to turn that bathroom into a place of warfare and breakthrough and make the devil pay. I noticed as I've done this over the years, bathrooms started to become a place of miracles and salvation. Yes, bathrooms, the place the enemy meant for harm, have become a place of countless, heartwarming, devil-stomping breakthroughs. I now expect miracles whenever I go in a bathroom.

BATHROOM GOD STORIES

One of the first bathroom God stories I remember was in a cafe on the Sunshine Coast in Australia many years ago. I was going into the bathroom and a lady I didn't know followed me; well, she actually chased me, *really*—and started knocking on the stall door, asking me to pray for healing for her. I was like, "Um, sure. I'll be out in a moment." I prayed right there in the bathroom and she was overcome with God's power.

I've prayed with people in a lot of places, but I can't tell you the joy it gives me releasing healing in a bathroom. Every time it's a devil-stomping joy! Another time I walked into the bathroom at a pub and I saw a lady doubled over in pain. I immediately asked if I could pray, and to her amazement she was instantly healed. She couldn't believe I'd walked in when I did and that God healed her.

The day Billy Graham died and went to Heaven, Ben and I specifically went out to find people to share Jesus with as a practical way to honor his life. We were in a local restaurant, and I walked into the bathroom. Out of the blue, a lady in there started crying and asked me to pray for her family. As we prayed, she rededicated her life to Jesus. We prayed for her kids to encounter God, too. This has happened so many times now.

I know it may sound strange, but I keep "finding" unsuspecting people who need God "just waiting" in bathrooms for a God encounter! I now expect God encounters because I am determined bathrooms will be a place of victory in my life!

I'm reminded of the day I walked into the bathroom at my local supermarket in Texas, where I've prayed for a lot of people. I noticed a lady who was really upset, so I immediately asked if I could help and if I could pray for her. To my surprise, another lady in the bathroom started cheering loudly and said to the woman, "Yeah, you really want her to pray for you!" I recognized this woman as someone I'd prayed for before. Then she asked if she could pray with me too! That was a first, I've got to say—I had a bathroom healing team that day! :)

So that's what we did standing right there in the supermarket bathroom—we had a small prayer meeting with people coming in and out, including little kids who walked in and started cheering, and then wanted to pray too. We all laid hands on this lady as we started praying. It really was quite funny as the atmosphere in that bathroom became filled with joy and laughter while we prayed. The lady who was on staff at the supermarket gave me a hug, cried, and was quite visibly touched by God.

As soon as I finished praying, the woman who joined the "prayer team," asked for prayer for healing too. So right there in the bathroom I prayed again releasing God's love and healing. Her pain left right there in the supermarket restroom. Praise Jesus! And yay for divine payback!

Because my husband and I have prayed for so many people in our local cafe and supermarket, the staff actually ask us to pray for people. I walked in a few months ago and immediately after I walked through the front door, a staff member asked if I could pray for her friend who was shopping that day and was unwell. I waited as she went and found her friend, and then I prayed for her. Then the lady I was praying for grabbed another staff member and said I should pray for her. I did, right there in the middle of the entranceway.

One of the bathroom stories that touched my heart deeply was a lady I heard in a Walmart bathroom on her phone swearing her head off and shouting—she was very angry. At first I was thinking how rude this lady was, and then compassion for her *came* on me. I waited for her to finish her call and then said, "It sounds like you're having a hard day, can I pray blessing over you?" "Yes," was her immediate response.

As I prayed, God gave me words about her life and how He loved her. This lady who moments before was angry and fierce, was now crying in the middle of the bathroom, as people walked by. I asked her a simple question, "Would you like to invite Jesus into your heart and life?" Again, her answer was "Yes." We stood together hugging, praying, and crying together as Jesus met her, in a Walmart bathroom. She walked into a bathroom one way, and walked out a changed person. That bathroom became a place of salvation that day. A place of battle once again became a place of victory. Now that's warfare! That's divine payback. That's my Jesus.

One thing that really affected me about this story is that I was originally annoyed at this lady and judged her. I certainly wasn't thinking about her as being another God story waiting to happen. I think of this lady often, as that particular morning I heard the Holy Spirit whisper something to me, "Can I use you today? Can I send you?"

I replied, "Of course." I wondered how, and then I heard Him say, "I'll show you."

When compassion fell on me to pray for her, I realized that this was God saying, "This one, Jodie, this is where I'd like to use you today." Oh tears! To think I nearly missed this God moment right there in that bathroom. How kind of God to remind me to see people through His eyes, even in bathrooms.

SEND ME

God has only got one kind of harvester—the ones who say yes! I know I'm talking about bathroom stories, but that day in a store bathroom, I too had a God moment. I could hear the whisper of Jesus as we stood weeping in the bathroom, "Can I send you?" That day I renewed my yes. *"Here I am. Send me"* (Isaiah 6:8 NLT). It's an honor to be sent to the highways and the byways, and even the bathrooms, of the nations—to be the King's decree of hope.

What the devil has tried to steal from you, you will walk in an authority for a harvest of breakthroughs! Speak this over yourself. The purpose of what's come against you has always been to keep you from your destiny and prevent you from winning a harvest for Jesus in your sphere of influence.

What is your *"bathroom"* in your life? Where are the places the enemy has tried to limit, contain, and attack you? Where can you believe for a harvest of breakthroughs, where the enemy has stolen from you? Where can you call in divine payback? The devil's plan hasn't worked. You are rising stronger.

You are more than your story of hard days and challenging seasons. You are not defined by your circumstances—*you are defined only by the voice of God.* When you know this, whatever you are facing, you *will* walk with assurance that where your feet go, so does breakthrough.

Whether I'm praying for people in churches, revival meetings, in cafes, on the street, or in bathrooms, I am taking back what was stolen and purposing to walk in authority that is mine to walk in. Wherever *you* have been robbed, you too have biblical precedent to call in divine payback, upgrades of authority, and a harvest of breakthroughs. The God of breakthrough is fiercely speaking breakthrough over you, my friend.

I often specifically decree that I am getting back what the enemy has stolen, *and more.* There's an urgency to establish faith expectations with our decrees so that the enemy doesn't get the last word. The King's voice is the determining voice in our journey and our intercession is establishing God-change. Whether we are calling back promises into our own lives, others' lives, or our nations, the same truth applies. When the thief is found out, there is a sevenfold redemption to contend for in prayer. I feel the urgency of the season, that God is redeeming our stories and as a people we are arising into not-seen-before breakthroughs.

For instance, the enemy has messed with my health, as you know. I have decreed not just healing and health restored, but better than before. But it doesn't stop there, I decree that I walk in authority of breakthrough where the enemy has stolen from me. Hear this, friend—your journey doesn't disqualify you, it qualifies you! In the places where the enemy has attacked you the most, these are the areas you are called to carry the *most* anointing and breakthrough. So in health, I call back not only fullness of health, but a sevenfold increase of anointing and authority to decree healing in the nations! This is my divine payback. What's your divine payback look like? This makes the devil pay. This is fullness of restoration. This is divine upgrade. This shifts us from the accusation of victim, to the truth of victorious living.

VISION OF BOWS AND RIBBONS

While ministering in Houston, Texas, I had a vision of bows and ribbons being released from Heaven; as far as I could see, ribbons and bows everywhere. There were so many of them and they looked incredible, but it struck me that the gift wasn't attached to the bow and ribbon. It bothered me as I knew there was meant to be gifts attached to all the bows and ribbons that were being released to people and regions.

I asked the Lord, "Why are there no gifts?"

I immediately heard Him say, "I'm waiting for My people to *ask* Me"

Wow, did that hit home. There are unprecedented breakthroughs and answers to prayer awaiting the body, that must be called in by our decrees! God wants us to *ask!* I could hear the urging of the Lord saying to the body of Christ right now, "What do you want Me to do for you?"—just as Jesus asked the blind man. Clearly the man's need was obvious, and yet, clearly his voice in the very act of asking was equally crucial.

> *"What do you want me to do for you?" Jesus asked him. The blind man said, "Rabbi, I want to see"* (Mark 10:51).

Our voices are the determining factor in the unfolding story of our nations, destiny, and season of greater breakthrough than we've experienced before. There's an invitation to be specific, to be bold, to be who we are—ambassadors of the King—and decree and establish the Kingdom with the authority that we have already been given by our King. I hear Jesus asking us, "What do you want Me to do for you?" Our prayer, our decrees, and our voices are undeniably crucial in this season. Call back what the evil "robbing spirit" has stolen. Divine payback is your inheritance. Ask for nations. Ask for divine solutions. Ask for all God has for you.

You Are Rising Out of Your Desert

I can sense the tenderness of God cheering you on and urging you to advance boldly, friend. This is the season you have been waiting for. *You* are rising out of your desert! I love the words of Song of Solomon 8:5-7. I believe they are a prophetic love song over the Church right now, speaking life and promise and declaring promise of redemption to you in this season.

> *Who is this one? Look at her now! She arises out of her desert, clinging to her beloved* (Song of Solomon 8:5 TPT).

God is reminding you to take a look for a moment at the journey you have walked and how far you have come. What incredible strength and courage you have exhibited as you have continued to stand, continued to believe, continued to serve the King, continued to contend and put your hope in His name.

I hear the Father saying to His Church, "WHO IS THIS ONE? LOOK AT HER NOW! SHE ARISES OUT OF HER

DESERT!" I love that this doesn't say, *the* desert, but *her* desert. Whatever desert *you* have walked through, has come against you, or tried to steal life from you—*you are rising out of your desert!* Look how far you've come.

You are not the same as you once were, you have journeyed long and far, but all that you have faced, every time the enemy thought he finally stopped you—look at you now! Rivers of pain and persecution have not extinguished your flame, endless floods were unable to quench your burning after Him. You are arising out of your desert, a champion of the King with His seal of fire fastened to your heart. The King is brooding over you and celebrating your courage. You are arising out of your desert and impacting the nations.

Read the following words from Song of Solomon as a prophetic proclamation over your next season from the Father. Read this as the King's decree to your heart:

> *Who is this one? Look at her now! She arises out of her desert, clinging to her beloved. When I awakened you under the apple tree, as you were feasting upon me, I awakened your innermost being with the travail of birth as you longed for more of me. Fasten me upon your heart as a seal of fire forevermore. This living, consuming flame will seal you as my prisoner of love. My passion is stronger than the chains of death and the grave, all consuming as the very flashes of fire from the burning heart of God. Place this fierce, unrelenting fire over your entire being. Rivers of pain and persecution will never extinguish this flame. Endless floods will be unable to quench this raging fire that burns within you. Everything will be consumed. It will stop at nothing as you yield everything to this*

furious fire until it won't even seem to you like a sacrifice anymore (Song of Solomon 8:5-7 TPT).

THE KING'S DECREE FOR YOU

"My child, I am bringing full restoration into every area that the thief has stolen from you. I am decreeing redemption, divine payback, and full restoration over your life. My love for you is unrelenting."

—THE KING

MY PRAYER FOR YOU

I'm praying for you now, friend, and I call you faithful, persevering, courageous, and honored by the King. I am praying full redemption in every place the thief has robbed you, and I call in divine restitution, restoration, and reward. I decree you will walk in chain-breaking authority in your life, to release a harvest of breakthrough in the very places the enemy has sought to rob you. You are rising in fierce faith; and your voice, your very life is anointed by the King as one He can trust to bring others out of their grave circumstances. I am praying that you too will experience resurrection life, turnarounds, and miracles in your current circumstances that stomp on the enemy's schemes. I speak an impartation of revival fire, faith for now, breakthrough and contagious hunger after God increasing in your life. You are walking out of the battle not only victorious, but with a harvest of souls, miracles, and triumphs around you. I bless you, mighty one. In Jesus' name, amen.

DECREE

- I will receive divine payback for all the enemy has stolen.
- I increasingly walk in victory and authority in the areas I have been attacked, and I release this to others.
- I am walking in authority, upgrades, and increase.
- God redeems all things in my life.
- I say yes to every promise God has for my life. I am His harvester. I am His sent one.

Chapter 18

YOU ARE THE KING'S DECREE

You yourselves write a decree concerning the Jews, as you
please, in the king's name, and seal it with the king's
signet ring; for whatever is written in the king's name
and sealed with the king's signet ring no one can revoke.
—ESTHER 8:8 NKJV

You are, the King's decree. Your life, your voice, your journey speaks on behalf of the King. Every breakthrough, your victories large and small, every time you take the King at His word and just keep standing and releasing light to the darkness, you are testifying on behalf of the King. Your courageous story speaks freedom to captives, peace to storms, life to dry bones, possible to impossible, Heaven to earth, truth to confusion, salvation to the lost, miracles to the hurting, and hope to the broken. By living this, you become the King's decree on earth. Where your feet tread, darkness shudders because you carry the King within you. When your voice proclaims life, all creation listens. This is who you are.

I love how Esther 8:8 says, *"You yourselves write a decree...as you please!"* King Ahasuerus was speaking to Esther and Mordecai and giving them authority to issue a decree on his behalf. In the NIV translation it says, *"as seems best to you."* The king was giving full authority to decree on his behalf. Our King, the King of kings and God Almighty, does the same. We have authority to speak forth declarations on behalf of the King because when we are surrendered to Him, He trusts us with His authority. What a privilege. What an honor.

You are a living signet ring in the hand of the King with permission to sign decrees on earth. What you decree as you partner with the King of kings cannot be revoked by the schemes of the enemy.

No wonder all *"creation waits in eager expectation for the children of God to be revealed"* (Romans 8:19). There are breakthroughs you will release as you decree and establish a thing, with the authority that has come from courageously walking through the fire and your clothes not even smelling like smoke. Not only does your voice speak, but your testimony, your very life speaks to a world that is watching. You have become an instrument of hope and releaser of resurrection life in the hand of your King.

SPEAK TO THE ROCK

*You and Aaron must take the staff and assemble the entire community. As the people watch, **speak to the rock** over there, and it will pour out its water. You will provide* *enough water from the rock to satisfy the whole community and their livestock* (Numbers 20:8 NLT).

I keep hearing in my spirit over and over, *"Speak to the rock."* As we enter this new era of accelerated change, harvest, and breakthrough, God is emphasizing the need to speak forth and decree what He is saying, establishing God-change, and writing future history with decrees of faith. I sense prophetic, strategic wisdom on this instruction to *speak to the rock*.

When the Israelites were thirsty in the wilderness, two times Moses was instructed to bring water from the rock for them, one time at the start of their forty-year journey, the second time at the end of their epic forty-year journey. The first time, God said *strike* the rock and water will pour out and it did (Exodus 17). The second time was just before entering the Promised Land and all that this represented. But this time God said, *"speak to the rock."* Same scenario, but different divine strategy.

What unfolds is really sad, as Moses gets angry with the people and strikes the rock twice instead of speaking to the rock. Amazingly, the rock still poured out water for the nation, but God tells Moses that because he didn't trust Him and speak to the rock, he would not enter the new season with the rest of the nation. It interests me that God said it was lack of trust in Him that prevented Moses from speaking to the rock. God was highlighting the importance of trusting, obeying, and decreeing to enter the new.

As God is releasing strategic wisdom that is custom-made for this next season, last season's strategies will just not work in the same way. The Lord is saying that as we enter this new era, the strategies to breakthrough and harvest are changing. That where we struck the rock, we now must *speak* to the rock. Our mouths, voices, and decrees are being amplified. It follows that a re-establishing of a plumb line of holiness and fear of the Lord is increasing, as authority on our voice is increasing. Our intercession and declarations will carry greater authority as our decrees align earth to Heaven's heart and release "living water" to the nations. We are living declarations from the King to those around us.

In this new era, we will be stewarding unprecedented Promised Land harvest. We are being given upgraded authority to steward fulfilled promises and increasing breakthrough. We are being upgraded to steward abundance of harvest instead of surviving in lack. The strategies are shifting and our voices are powerful in this process. We are invited to make decrees on the King's behalf as "it seems best" to us and the King—which assumes a level of intimacy with the King. Wow, that's authority to steward in the fear of the Lord! No wonder God is urging us, just as He did with Moses, to *speak to the rock* as we are entering a new season of fulfilled promise with upgraded authority to evict giants.

You are entering *your* promised land, friend—*speak* to the rock, open your mouth and declare His word—expect miracle solutions to flow, and decree God's promises as fiery weapons seeding and writing in faith your future victories. The world awaits the Church that is arising now. For truly, our faith-filled decrees are rewriting darkness to light, chaos to order, division to unity, hatred to love, and hopeless fear to hope-filled hearts that in the manifest presence of God, our King Jesus has solutions.

As we arise out of our desert, we carry something precious, an inner confidence that the King is our Friend. And there is no more precious gift than to be friends with the King of kings. Our friendship and journey with Jesus has made our voices powerful. Our voices decree on behalf of the King. It's even more than that though, because it's more than words, it's more than what we do or say—our very lives are the message. Our hard-fought-for faith is the proclamation of breakthrough. Everything we've walked through with our King makes our decrees even more powerful. Our very lives are a decree of victory and provoke change.

There are Marys Everywhere

While in the hospital some time ago, I met a lady whose story deeply touched me. I had four drains coming out of my body, including one in my nose that was particularly uncomfortable as it made it hard to breath and talk. I was feeling a bit down and close to tears from the pain on this particular morning, so Ben and I were going to the hospital lounge room to get me away from the room for a minute and to clear my head.

I looked at a lady sitting there in a wheelchair and she looked so sick and depressed. I knew I needed to pray for her even though, honestly, it was the last thing I felt like doing. Ben and I prayed. She was thankful, but not very responsive. Nevertheless, I was glad I'd prayed. I had discovered her name was Mary, she was in her 80s and had terminal cancer. She was particularly upset because she had never been away from her husband in their fifty-plus years of marriage. She kept saying, "I just want to go home." I was really touched by her story.

I eventually shuffled back to my hospital room, but as I sat on my bed, I couldn't stop thinking about this lady. She was weighing heavy on my heart and so I was really interceding for her. The more I prayed for her, the more she weighed heavy on my heart. Suddenly I looked at Ben and said, "I've got to find Mary." Her desire to just go home was making me cry as I realized Mary wanted to go home, but I knew what she really needed was to know Jesus. I knew she couldn't "go home," as she had never invited Jesus into her life. I felt the urgency of telling her and knew I was entrusted with an assignment from God.

I had no idea where Mary's room was, but I took off on a mission, slowly shuffling, and found her sitting in a room not too far from mine. Thankfully she was alone. She was being fed through a tube and was skin and bones, so I knew things where serious.

I boldly walked in and said, "Mary, do you remember me?"

"Yes," she said.

I explained that I couldn't stop thinking about her and God had sent me back to talk to her. I explained how Jesus loved her and wanted her to have an eternal home with Him one day, and that I was sent to ask her if she wanted to invite God into her life today.

Mary didn't say yes right away, she actually just looked at me like I was wasting my time and told me she wasn't "religious." I was not put off, I felt the compassion of God and the urgency of the moment.

I explained again that God had sent me to her to ask her this and to tell her that He loved her. I could feel the battle going on internally. A nurse walked in and seemed annoyed I was there, so I started praying under my breath. I knew God had put Mary on my heart.

As soon as the nurse left, I boldly asked again, "Mary, would you like to invite Jesus into your heart and life and let God make a home in you?" She sighed the biggest, longest sigh and bowed her head, like she was letting go of decades of struggle. Then she looked at me and quietly said, "Yes."

In that moment in her hospital room with tubes everywhere in both of us, we cried as we prayed a simple prayer together and her hospital room became a place of victory. I then shuffled back to my room. I never saw Mary again, but I know I'll see her in eternity.

The only time our circumstances can define us is when we let them. Hospitals, bathrooms, mountaintops or valleys—whatever we have walked through or are walking through, we are ambassadors from the King. I may have been in the hospital, but I was the King's decree for Mary that day.

A powerful truth we all carry is, it's not what comes against us or what valleys we have traveled through that characterizes our lives, it's how we respond and rise above that makes the difference. The hope we release in the darkest of valleys shouts praise to the King and speaks into eternity that our Jesus is worthy, no matter what—always.

There are many "Marys" everywhere—people who need an encounter with a loving God. Whether I'm speaking to someone in a hospital, a bathroom, in another nation, down the road, or from a platform, people are the same everywhere—just a child of God who needs to know how to find their way back home to the King's love, their heavenly Father. Just as I was the King's decree for Mary, *you are* the King's decree for those to whom God sends you. Nations await what you carry. Speak to the rocks and mountains in your world, and release what God has placed within you.

Mark our hearts, Jesus, to live to hear You say, "Well done good and faithful servant." As I've said, this thought drives my life. I also live with great awareness of His grace, for which I'm deeply thankful He gives us all. But I often think about that day when I will finally see Jesus, and I wonder, will I say, "I wish I gave You more."

I think I will. *This* thought *always makes me cry*. It's raw and it's real. He is worthy of my more.

FEAST ON HOPE

You may have dealt with unimaginable tragedy. You may have fought through unthinkable challenges. You may have achieved what once seemed insurmountable mountaintop victories. And now, what seemed a ceiling not long ago, has become the platform to climb even higher. You've faced paralyzing fears in the valley of the shadow, and you came out evicting fear's hold and feasting on hope. You truly are unstoppable as although you paid a price, nothing the enemy has thrown at you has kept you down. Attempts to muzzle, squash, and intimidate your voice have only strengthened your courage.

There are prayers you have yet to pray that will change nations and impact lives you don't even know yet. There are inventions, projects, messages, and movements in you that will speak to the multitudes and speak to the one in front of you. We all have a kingdom assignment, a race to run, a lane that is ours. The baton is being handed from glory to glory; and just as Heaven is cheering you on, let *your* words cheer on others too. Sometimes, indeed often, breakthrough is but one anointed, courageous declaration away. Be the mouthpiece of divine encouragement and catalyst of supernatural solutions that "speaks to the rock."

My prayer is simple as I finish these pages that I have prayed breakthrough over every word. May you know your life is an edict from the King, that nothing is impossible and that hope, *supernatural* hope, never runs out. Everything you've walked through, the great, the good, the bad, and the ugly, may all of it only serve to solidify your decree, *"I can do all things through Christ who strength-ens me"* (Philippians 4:13 NKJV).

All Heaven celebrates you, and God believes in you. I am com-pelled to urge you to release what is on your life, my friend. These are the days you are made for and God dreamed of as He saw who you were created to be, before you were even born. You carry within you a mandate from Heaven that is custom-made for you, and needed right now, where God has placed you.

> *You saw who you created me to be before I became me!*
> (Psalm 139:16 TPT)

Your challenges and journey are different from mine, but the same King is cheering us both on. The same King believes in us and says, "I'm sending you as a message to *your* world." Through your life, the Redeemer lives. Your voice is anointed with the authority of the King to speak words that only you can say, and release break-throughs that only you carry. The King looks and sees a harvest of souls, and He also looks and sees His beloved bride arising victo-riously, decreeing His goodness. He is urging all of us, "Speak, I AM with you."

I want you to hear this truth *again,* friend, as it's worthy of receiving deep in your soul, so it echoes in you beyond this book and impacts throughout your life. Take a moment, breathe, and then let the following decree brand you—with a seal of fire, from the King.

You are The King's Decree. Your life, your voice, and your journey speaks on behalf of the King. Every breakthrough, every victory large and small, every time you take the King at His word and just keep standing, releasing light to the darkness, you are testify-ing on behalf of the King. Your courageous story speaks freedom to captives, peace to storms, life to dry bones, possible to impossible, Heaven to earth, truth to confusion, salvation to the lost, miracles to the hurting, hope to the broken. You literally become the King's decree on the earth. Where your feet tread, darkness shudders because you carry the King within you. When your voice proclaims life, all creation listens. This is who you are.

You are the most precious, most valuable, most contended for, most loved, most powerful of all God's creations—and you, yes *you*—are *The King's Decree*.

THE KING'S DECREE FOR YOU

"My child, YOU ARE MY DECREE. You are my greatest decree on earth. I have given you all authority to speak in My name and be My living signet ring to the world around you. I love you, endlessly."

—THE KING

MY PRAYER FOR YOU

I am praying for you right now and decreeing life, life, life in Jesus' name. I decree increase on your voice, favor on your message, and breakthrough on your destiny. I honor your heart after the King and the way you have sought the Lord even when it has cost you. I am praying that as you finish reading these pages, the fire that has been ignited continues to burn fiercely. I speak blessing and anointing on all that God calls you to.

As you go, I pronounce breakthrough. As you go, I pronounce you yourself are the edict of hope that others read, and the decree of the King that others encounter. I pray a fire in you that never goes out and bless you to walk with your friend, King Jesus, all the days of your life.

I may never know you on earth, friend, but one day, I will meet you in eternity. Until then, I bless your journey with the manifest glory of God. You are truly the most precious, most valuable, most contended for, most powerful and most loved of all God's creations. I pray blessing as you go and be The King's Decree in your world. In Jesus' name, amen.

DECREE

- I am the King's decree. My voice and my journey speak on behalf of the King. I speak freedom to captives, peace to the storm, life to dry bones, the impossible made possible, Heaven to earth, truth to confusion, salvation to the lost, miracles to the hurting, and hope to the broken.

- I am a living signet ring in the hand of the King.

- I walk as the decree of the King to the world around me. My voice proclaims life, and where my feet tread, darkness shudders.

- I AM THE KING'S DECREE!

ABOUT THE AUTHOR

Jodie and Ben Hughes are the founders of Pour It Out Ministries and have been in ministry together for more than twenty years. They, along with their adult daughter Keely, travel full time around the world as Revivalists, with an emphasis on breakthrough, prophetic declaration, healing, and preaching the gospel with miracles, signs, and wonders following in their personal lives and ministry endeavors. Ministering as a family imparts great hope and relatability to many.

They are known for hosting the eighteen-month Pineapple Revival in Australia, which saw many thousands come from around the world to attend. As well as being full-time itinerant Revivalists and prophets, they have pastored and planted several churches, trained thousands of ministry students in their schools, recorded worship albums, and authored prophetic insight articles and blogs.

Jodie pioneered and leads Mentor Me, an international online mentoring program, and regularly releases prophetic words and mentoring wisdom. She is an engaging speaker and influencer known for being real, inspiring hope, imparting contagious hunger, and transferable revival fire.

Originally from Australia, they are based in Texas, USA. Visit their website at: www.pouritout.org